Infectious Innovation

Infectious Innovation

Secrets of Transforming Employee Ideas into Dramatic Revenue Growth

James Allan

BEP BUSINESS EXPERT PRESS

Infectious Innovation: Secrets of Transforming Employee Ideas into Dramatic Revenue Growth

First published in 2017 by
Business Expert Press, LLC
222 East 46th Street, New York, NY 10017
www.businessexpertpress.com

ISBN-13: 978-1-94709-851-0 (paperback)
ISBN-13: 978-1-94709-852-7 (e-book)

Business Expert Press Human Resource Management and Organizational Behavior Collection

Collection ISSN: 1946-5637 (print)
Collection ISSN: 1946-5645 (electronic)

Cover and interior design by Exeter Premedia Services Private Ltd., Chennai, India

First edition: 2017

10 9 8 7 6 5 4 3 2 1

Printed in the United States of America.

Abstract

How do you make innovation a core competency of your business?

This book details a process to allow innovation to seep into your company's culture. It outlines the steps necessary to generate, collect, triage, escalate, and pilot ideas which are necessary to optimize a company's chance at success with new products, services, and processes.

After explaining steps of the process in detail, *Infectious Innovation* outlines feedback mechanisms so business leaders can continually get better at making innovation a success!

Keywords

idea generation, infectious innovation, infectious innovation index, innovation, innovation management, new processes, new products, new services, pilot, predictable innovation, revenue growth, successful innovation

Contents

Testimonial

"It's an incredibly useful tool for business professionals and executives looking to foster innovation and creativity in their companies and employees."

—Courtney Symons, Partner Marketing Manager, Shopify.

"Infectious Innovation is a valuable playbook for executives to harness the creativity of their organizations to drive sustainable innovation. Paired with an approach to gain fresh perspective on the disruptive forces of our time, and you have a framework for a solid innovation strategy that will deliver dividends."

—Brendan Byrne, MD, Firstep Innovations, Chief Innovation Officer
TELUS Health.

CHAPTER 1

Why Innovation Now? (When the Wind is Blowing, Raise the Sails)

Market leaders need innovation to sustain their lead. Disruptors need innovation to become market leaders. While organizations in all industries need innovation, few business leaders are creating ecosystems that are able to grow and cultivate innovation. Meanwhile, employees in these organizations are coming up with ideas daily on how to create and sustain growth. But these ideas aren't being heard, or aren't being acted upon. So, while any business leader will tell you people are their most important resource, they're lying! They always prefer to go outside their organization to come up with big ideas that can help create and sustain revenue growth.

Since innovation is necessary, and an organization's people are its most important resource, *Infectious Innovation* will teach you how to systematically collect employee ideas, and then turn them into improved and sustainable profits.

Intent

The intent of *Infectious Innovation: Secrets of Transforming Employee Ideas into Dramatic Revenue Growth* is to do exactly that: to explain to business leaders how to set up processes within their organization to turn employee ideas into actionable tasks. These tasks will then serve to dramatically increase company revenues.

Personal development experts continue to say, "Work smart, not hard." Meanwhile, organizations are focusing far too much on the productivity side of the equation. They are working hard, not smart. The upstarts, which are run by the new generation of business leaders, are realizing that organizations may work smarter by encouraging their staff to innovate.

Changes

The more things change, the more they stay the same. The business world, as we know it, is similar in many ways today to what it was 60 years ago. Some businesses sell products and services to consumers, and some sell products and services to other businesses. Money, ideas, and people are the inputs for all businesses. Even children selling lemonade on a street corner need all three—money to purchase supplies, ideas to help decide when and where to sell the lemonade, and people to make and sell the lemonade.

The difference today is not the functions of business, but rather the form. Sixty years ago, money came in the form of cash or check. Today, cash and checks are usually acceptable, but so too is electronic transfer.

Sixty years ago, ideas were created using imagination and education. Education was from local radio, television, and newspapers and libraries, as well as from friends and family. Today, all three sources are available, as well as an online library with access to more information than one could read in their lifetime.

Sixty years ago, people in a business were needed to produce, deliver, and sell goods and services. As well, people were needed for finance, general, and administrative duties in order to ensure the business was making the best use of its money and people. Today, the same units are still needed.

While the general structure of a business has not changed significantly in the last 60 years (see Figure 1.1), the contents have changed dramatically. The value in most organizations 60 years ago came from tangible goods, while the value in most organizations today comes from intangible goods.

While a lot of the focus has come from new products, new services, new technologies, and new delivery methods, there continues to be pressure on revenue and profit growth.

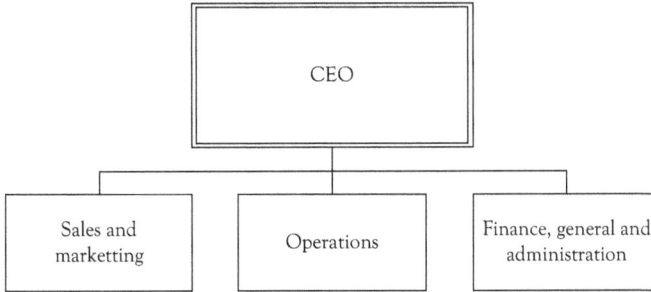

Figure 1.1 Traditional organizational structure

Everybody is interested in growth. Senior management has bonuses associated with revenue and profit growth. Meanwhile, investors are looking for growth. In public companies, shareholders are looking for revenue and profit growth. With so many options available for purchasing stocks, an accessible global market, and an increasing demand on workers to look after their own retirement, shareholders expect growth or will sell their shares. Similarly, employees want to work for a company that is growing.

With senior management, investors, shareholders, and employees looking for growth, businesses need to grow!

In order to grow, what is needed? Since most global markets have been exhausted, innovation is the answer.

What Is Innovation?

Innovation is defined in the *Merriam-Webster Dictionary* as "the introduction of something new" or "a new idea, method, or device." As this is a business book, the innovation being discussed here is innovation in relation to business. So a better definition as it relates to business innovation is "the introduction of something new in business" or "a new business product, service, customer relationship, or process."

Innovation itself is nothing new. Humankind has been creative since its early beginnings. The assembly line, the airplane, and the World Wide Web have been innovations over time with dramatic impacts.

Attitudes toward innovation have been all over the map. Some people love innovation, while others are fearful. Some people profit from new innovations, while others suffer due to them. Automation has helped business leaders get their product to market faster with higher quality, but it has also put the people who previously performed the manual labor out of work.

In terms of business innovation, "the introduction of something new" may range from something small to something enormous. For the purposes of this book, "incremental innovation" refers to small changes while "explosive innovation" refers to large-scale changes. An example of incremental innovation might be a cell phone manufacturer upgrading their camera from a 32-megapixel to a 64-megapixel format. An example of explosive innovation might be a cell phone manufacturer moving into the development of financial software that helps sell more cell phones.

A business innovation, in terms of this book, refers to the introduction of something new to the organization that is introducing it. For example, currently there are many players in the autonomous vehicle industry. Blackberry announced recently it would be developing autonomous cars. This was not an industry innovation, but it was a business innovation since it was a new direction for Blackberry.

A business innovation needs to be something which is commercially available. It is quite different from an invention or an unused patent. New technology is not a business innovation until it is successfully commercialized. An invention is merely a product or service that may have some future purpose.

Best Time Ever to Innovate

Innovation excites many people, but causes skepticism amongst others. No matter which side of the fence you're on, NOW is the best time ever to innovate. With current technology to drive change, and the current state of communications and social media to help business leaders stay on top of changes, the barrier to entry of businesses for innovation is smaller than ever. Small companies can start prototyping and grow to scale quickly. Innovators that have been financially successful are looking to help other innovators to grow quickly.

Today, the cost of introducing and commercializing innovation is less than it was 40 years ago. In the '70s, five-sixths of the S&P 500 value was in tangible goods. Nowadays, that number has been flipped on its head. Five-sixths of the S&P 500 value is now in intangible goods. So the cost of materials and manufacturing has been greatly reduced for today's innovations.

How companies incorporate innovation into their product streams has changed over the years. Large companies used to live off their fat. They would allow small companies to innovate, and then grow by acquiring the innovative small companies once they had proved their business model. This has changed dramatically over the last 20 years! The four largest companies in terms of market capitalization, Apple, Microsoft, Amazon, and Google/Alphabet, have become the most innovative. Apple has launched itself into the financial technology (fintech) sector with Apple Pay, while Amazon became a successful product manufacturer (well outside its main business stream) with the introduction of Alexa. Google renamed itself to Alphabet to represent the depth and breadth of its business ventures, and Microsoft continues to come out with business innovations.

Old-world companies are innovating to stay relevant. Lego was a toy that young people loved to play with before the video game era. While children (of all ages) continue to enjoy Lego, the organization has greatly expanded its brand to include movies and theme parks. It also has created a business strategy empire with its Lego Serious Play workshops. Consultants can be certified facilitators of the workshops, which help executives use Lego pieces to improve teamwork and develop new strategies.

Ideas lead to innovation, but innovation success does not depend on being the first to have the idea. The most successful innovators were usually not the first to have an idea. Google was not the first search engine. Facebook was not the first social media site. Yet Google and Facebook were able to become extremely successful by taking their innovations further than their competitors.

It's never too late to innovate, despite what mature companies may think. When I was in my early twenties, I was playing rugby every weekend. One Saturday, our captain, who happened to be the smallest player on the field, was tackled aggressively. He was lying immobile on the ground and it wasn't looking good for him. The referee blew the whistle, and we went running over to see how he was doing. One of the spares on the sidelines started warming up since he figured our captain could not continue playing. The trainer came over to look at him, and was hopeful since the captain was fairly alert, though not moving. The coach called over to the spare to come in, and the captain said, "Hey! I'm not dead yet." He got up and continued to play.

If your business is still active, then it's not too late to innovate and thrive. Never give up.

Every industry is capable of innovating, not just the high-tech industries that rely exclusively on an ever-increasing landscape of new technology. In my hometown, the construction industry is continually innovating to offer better products and services in less time. The abundance of technology advancements has created opportunities for innovation in every industry out there. That is why the Internet of Things (IoT) is becoming so mainstream. Everything, from household appliances to security systems to cell phones, is now connected and communicating.

With increasing innovation, market demands are evolving. Paradigms from the twentieth century are being abandoned for new world thinking. An example is the increasing demand for entertainment since it is now accessible anywhere, which wasn't the case 20 years ago. Similarly, communication needs are always increasing as more and more people adopt cell phones and carry communication devices everywhere they go.

Just because innovation is all around us, does this mean all innovation is bound to be successful and eliminate the methods it's replaced? Absolutely not. In the 1930s, there was research done to improve on the QWERTY keyboard, which is still the standard today (it is so named because the first six letters on the top left of the keyboard are QWERTY). A man named Dvorak came up with a better keyboard that studies showed allowed people to type much faster and avoid hand problems (see Figure 1.2). While people appreciated the fact that the studies were true, inertia kept them using the QWERTY keyboard, and the Dvorak keyboard became a footnote in the history of better innovations that never caught on.

In the mid-1980s, the banking industry introduced the method of collecting and distributing money through automated tellers. Thirty years later, there are still many people who use the human bank tellers to deposit and withdraw money, and have chosen to avoid the automated teller innovation.

Despite the risks of innovation, governments at all levels are looking to help business leaders innovate. They want their economy to do well,

Figure 1.2 The Dvorak keyboard was proven to be superior

and innovation has been seen to be a major contributor to help employment levels. There is innovation funding available for incubators in most large cities. While Silicon Valley remains the mecca for innovation, many other cities are trying to copy its success. Many Canadian cities, including Calgary, the Toronto-Waterloo corridor, and Ottawa, call themselves Silicon Valley North in hopes of attracting good investment and good employees.

Innovation is never easy, especially explosive innovation. New products often require new policies. Autonomous vehicles, for example, require a new way of looking at insurance, licensing, and law enforcement. Policy makers want to have the policies in place before allowing the autonomous vehicles on the road.

Although innovation has its negative side, NOW is the best time for businesses in all industries to innovate.

More Important than Ever

Innovation is more important now than it's ever been. Everyone is looking for growth companies.

With millions of baby boomers nearing retirement age to lead the way, investment dollars are being thrown into growth companies. Your company had better be growing! Shareholders are looking for their investments to grow, and the best way to grow is through innovation.

Employees are also looking for companies that are growing. In the early '80s, layoffs demonstrated a lack of employer loyalty. This in turn has created a lack of employee loyalty over the last 30 years. In order to keep the best employees, organizations need to continue to grow, and business innovation is the best tool for growth.

Many businesses, even industries, have disappeared over the years. Phone books used to be a staple in every home. The movie "The Intern" poked fun at how the 70-year-old character, portrayed by Robert De Niro, used to work in the same building that he is now a senior intern at. The protagonist had worked in the building for 30 or 40 years when it housed a telephone book manufacturer, but the building had been repurposed to house an online fashion start-up.

While the businesses have disappeared, in many cases the function of the business hadn't changed. It was the form of the business that had changed. In the phone book example, the function was to have a method people could use to find out how to contact friends, family, and merchants by telephone. That function didn't change; rather its form was transformed from a paper telephone book to a software app.

In order to continue to grow, business leaders should be looking at the functions the business is providing, and try to determine what the form will be like in the next few years. Blockbuster was the market leader in the '90s, by far, for video rentals. According to *Netflixed*, Blockbuster correctly identified that the video rental market was switching to an electronic delivery system, yet they felt too attached to their brick-and-mortar stores to make the proper investment in an electronic delivery system.

Meanwhile, as some industries adopt new innovations, related industries need to innovate to adapt. An example is the software support industry. When personal computers became available and popular in the '80s, owners of the personal computers were looking for software. The standard business model was that software would be sold on a one-time basis. As the hardware supporting the software rapidly improved, the software industry would upgrade their software for the newest hardware. This was also true with business software. In the late '80s, and through much of the '90s, computers were doubling their capacity every two years or so. So new, upgraded software was always being offered to work with the newer hardware. Businesses would not always be quick to get the latest and greatest software and hardware as soon as it was offered. When new software and hardware were purchased, businesses built support mechanisms to roll out the new software and hardware.

These support mechanisms were well-oiled machines for over 20 years as new software and hardware could be rolled out together. Then software providers started to realize that the banks had a great business model: Collect monthly subscription fees, paying which becomes habitual for clients. This software subscription model is known as Software as a Service (SaaS), and has many benefits to the end user. The support teams, however, have been forced to create innovations in their processes since the software companies can now roll out upgrades at any time, and support staffs have to prepare for them differently than before.

In a similar vein, the autonomous vehicle is an explosive innovation on the horizon, and has many businesses investing lots of money into it. The innovation offers benefits to vehicles that currently require humans to control. The trucking, shipping, taxi, and tractor companies are investigating how to innovate their business models to take advantage of the coming autonomous vehicle innovations. The companies which don't innovate will be left behind.

There are also other industries looking to take advantage of the autonomous vehicle innovation. Telecommunication companies have been investigating the ability of cars to communicate with other cars, pedestrians, and the city's infrastructure. Communicating with other cars and pedestrians will increase vehicle and pedestrian safety, while communicating with the city's infrastructure has the potential to give the city feedback on traffic and road issues that require attention.

Even if a certain industry itself is not innovating, organizations in the industry can take advantage of other innovations to improve their market share. This is another reason why it's so important that employees are given the chance to contribute to new products and services. There are so many innovations these days in so many industries, that it's hard for a small team to keep up with them all. Employees at all levels should be given the chance to contribute their ideas. This will increase the organization's ability to build on other innovations occurring around them.

Sometimes the friends or spouses of employees work at companies that are innovating, and the employees see a correlation between what the other companies are doing and how their own organization can innovate from it. These employees have voices that need to be heard!

Game Changers—Every Organization has them

Every organization has people with great ideas. There are the discontented who are never satisfied with current products and services. There are the dreamers who spend their time dreaming of a better service or product. And there are the inventors who are constantly trying new things to see what will happen. Every company has them, and they can be in any department.

Usually, the discontented employees, the dreamers, and the inventors come up with ideas to improve the organization but keep the ideas to themselves. There is no mechanism to forward their ideas to the "people that matter," so they mope or dream or continue to invent their own widgets in isolation. Wouldn't it be wonderful if there were a mechanism to gather their ideas and filter them down to the one or two that could make a difference? Imagine the effect it would have on the organization's bottom line if employees were able to have their ideas heard, and then see one or two of these ideas go into production.

One of the reasons some organizations fear asking and encouraging employees to come up with revenue-generating ideas is that the employees might generate the ideas on company time, and then leave to start their own business based on those ideas.

This fear is possible, but highly improbable. So why wouldn't employees with all these wonderful ideas just go and start businesses around these great ideas themselves? Some do, but most don't. There are many reasons why an employee would be much happier sharing their ideas with their employer than starting their own business.

Having a great idea and running a business built on a great idea are two wildly different things. Sure the lady in the packaging department can figure out a better way of getting products out the door, but it's a huge leap from telling people your wonderful idea to turning the idea into a new product or service.

If an organization's employee decides to start a business of her own, then she would have to find sales and distribution channels, in addition to developing and perfecting a new idea and service. Then there are financing and customer service to worry about; and let's not forget about product development!

The beauty of employees contributing ideas to their organization so that the organization can grow is that the organization already has the infrastructure to grow much more quickly. There are already customers, sales channels, and distribution networks that can get a new product or service to market quickly. There are also development teams that are able to turn ideas into movable products.

It's a perfect mix: Creative employees and organizations that want to grow!

Employees also have a vested interest in their organization growing. While experts will tell you that new grads expect to move companies every five years, there is also a need for stability that many employees desire. Nobody wants to work on a sinking ship. When I worked with one of my clients, Costco Wholesale, their employee retention rates were phenomenal. The company rep told me that 93 percent of employees that make it through the first three months will still be there after five years.

It's exciting when revenues are climbing and company leaders are excited. It's exciting when you work in sales and can tell your customers about new products coming down the pipe.

Early in my career, I worked at Newbridge Networks, a telecommunications firm. Every three months, the company's CEO, Terry Matthews, would give a quarterly report to all the employees. It was exciting to hear of the continual growth, and the CEO's tone would motivate the staff to continue to work hard to meet increasing customer demand.

When an organization adopts a culture of innovation, the employees appreciate it. Many employees will want to get and stay involved in the company's growth as much as they can. It's up to the organization to allow them the opportunity.

How can you spot a game changer? It's often more difficult than you would think. I once worked with a woman at a high-tech firm who had short black hair. Each month, she would paint a stripe down the middle of her hair in a different color. One month, the stripe would be white. The next month, it would be yellow. She seemed like the creative, out-of-the-box thinker that could come up with revolutionary ideas. If she was, she certainly wasn't the type to share her ideas with anybody.

I've also worked with the most conservative young people you could imagine that had the wildest ideas on earth. You never know who has great business innovation ideas, which is why you have to allow everyone to submit their ideas.

Conflicting and Compounding Innovations

As the number of innovations continues to increase, there become conflicting and compounding innovations. Conflicting innovations have caused problems for market leaders while compounding innovations have helped market leaders.

Over the years, conflicting innovations have caused many companies to lose their market lead. This occurs when new innovations conflict with their current business model.

Modern examples of industries that have been slow to adopt conflicting innovations are large retailers like Sears that were slow to adopt the online retailing model because it conflicted with their retail outlet model. They have suffered greatly as the market moved to online retailing without them.

An example cited above was Blockbuster, which recognized that online video rentals was an innovation that the market would need in the future, but this innovation conflicted with their current retail outlet model. They were leery of the new form of providing video rentals and went bankrupt due to their desire to stick with their current form.

Similarly, the railroad companies were in the business of transporting customers from one location to another. When airplanes came along as a new innovation, the railway companies should have recognized the market demand and evolved. Instead, they stuck with their current form.

Hopefully, organizations in the future will learn from mistakes in the past. They will look at innovations that may conflict with their current business model, and use them to their advantage, rather than try to compete against them.

Compounding innovations, on the other hand, can help market leaders keep or grow their lead. This occurs when an organization innovates while also using an innovation from another industry. An example is the Alexa product from Amazon. They were looking for an innovative new product to ease the buying process for Amazon customers. They came up with a voice recognition system that would sit in the middle of your home and allow you to order Amazon products by speaking. While this was one innovation on its own, the Alexa product compounded this with the ability to ask Alexa questions, and the ability of the voice recognition system to respond to voice commands within one second instead of the standard three seconds. The compounding of these innovations has helped Alexa to capture a huge market lead.

Compounding innovations has the effect of also compounding the risk. This in turn also has the effect of compounding the reward, which is often worth the risk.

Raising Hope: The Infectious Innovation Process

Employees looking for opportunities to get involved will be thrilled with the Infectious Innovation Process. The process allows them to contribute ideas to the growth of the company. It gives employees hope that their voice will be heard.

There is a television show entitled *Undercover Boss* where the CEO or other senior official in the company disguises themselves and works for the company at the staff level. For example, the CEO of a fast-food restaurant chain would work as a cashier at one of the organization's restaurants. At the end of the show, three or four staff members are rewarded for their hard work, and they almost always say the same thing, "It's good to be appreciated for the work you do. It seems like no one is ever watching."

Employees will be appreciated for contributing ideas. When other employees see the appreciation, they too will want to contribute.

Hope is a powerful thing. According to Greek mythology, the gods harnessed all the world's evils and put them in a box so that no evil would be present in the world. They feared that one day the box may be opened, so they placed at the bottom of the box the only thing that could combat evil: hope.

When Pandora opened the box, the world's evils were released and there was unrest for a while. But hope soon triumphed!

When employees have hope, they look forward to their day. They rush to work with excitement, and turn that excitement into energy.

Company growth gives employees hope. Permission to contribute gives employees hope. The Infectious Innovation Process allows companies to grow and gives permission to employees to contribute to that growth.

Over the next several chapters, the reader will see how the Infectious Innovation Process works, and what tools are available for the various stages. The five stages will be discussed in the chronological order in which they take place: Idea Generation, Idea Collection, Idea Triage, Idea Escalation, and the Pilot phase.

First, the Idea Generation stage will be discussed in Chapter 2. There are several methods to generate ideas, and then there are ways of capturing the ideas before they're lost. Chapter 3 discusses the Idea Collection stage. There are continual and finite methods to choose from. The Idea Triage stage is discussed in Chapter 4, outlining how ideas are grouped and then rated. Chapter 5 discusses the details of the Idea Escalation stage. The importance of senior management and the tools to outline the business value of each idea are described. Chapter 6 discusses the final stage of the Infectious Innovation Process, the Pilot. Selection criteria, location, and timing of the pilots are detailed. The final chapter of this book puts the whole process together. It then outlines tools that organizations can use to determine how well they are doing, and feedback mechanisms they can use to continually evolve their success with the Infectious Innovation Process.

Readers can use this book in many ways, and it depends where their organization ranks in the Infectious Innovation Index, as outlined in Chapter 7. If a reader is new to the Infectious Innovation Process, then every chapter should be read in order. This will give the reader a good idea on the various stages and how to optimize each stage.

As the reader incorporates the Infectious Innovation Process in their organization, all the stages should be studied first. The "Getting Started" section in Chapter 7 can then be used to incorporate the optimum timing and sequence of the various steps.

If a reader is already using the Infectious Innovation Process, but not getting the results they expected, and unsure where the problems are occurring, then Chapter 7 should be looked at first. It outlines feedback mechanisms that will help the reader determine where the current issues lie. After determining where the issues are, chapter summaries at the end of each chapter can be examined, to determine which specific chapters can be referred to on an as-needed basis.

Summary

What is Innovation?

- Definitions: innovation, incremental innovation versus explosive innovation
- Business innovation requires commercialization

Best Time Ever to Innovate

- NOW is the best time
- Innovation costs are lower with today's intangible goods
- Large companies are proving they are capable of innovating successfully

More Important than Ever

- Everyone—investors, shareholders, employees—is looking for growth companies
- Other industries are innovating, giving you opportunity to innovate

Every Organization has Game Changers

- The discontented, the dreamers, the inventors have ideas that can help
- Give them a voice

Conflicting and Compounding Innovations

- Conflicting innovations could hurt, while compounding innovations can help

Raising Hope

- Hope is a powerful tool that can excite employees
- Infectious Innovation Process gives employees hope

CHAPTER 2

Idea Generation (Secrets to Releasing Inner Creativity)

The first step for organizations to have ideas that may turn into dramatic profits is that staff members need to generate ideas. If we look at a visual form of the process, we see the process needs ideas to go into the Infectious Innovation Process funnel (see Figure 2.1). Ideas go into the top of the funnel, and increased revenues come out of the ideas that successfully make it through the entire funnel.

In order to be able to generate ideas, staff need time and space to free their mind to consider different possibilities. But how do they find time and space to generate ideas when today's organizations are asking their staff to produce more results with less people? How can employees feel comfortable about spending time generating and submitting ideas, when their performance is measured by their immediate results? These questions will be answered in this chapter.

Please note that this chapter is geared toward individual staff members generating their own ideas, and then getting together to share their ideas and collaborate with others. This is because team dynamics can often alter an individual's approach to new ideas. If, however, you are the type of person that believes you are more creative in a group than you are by yourself, feel free to apply these principles to an idea generation team of your own choosing.

Finding Time

Annual reviews are often centered on the outputs the employee has delivered during the year. In a results-based, competitive society, productivity is top of mind for many employees. Many companies are now conducting

Infectious innovation process

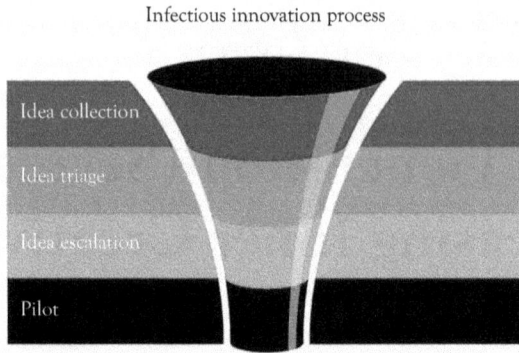

Figure 2.1 Infectious innovation process funnel

ongoing performance reviews, which further stresses to employees that immediate results outweigh long-term gain. In an effort to increase productivity, many employees often feel that it's imperative to fit as much working time into the day as possible.

These employees are making a huge mistake! Studies show that productivity is lower when fewer breaks are taken. The Draugiem Group, using a time-tracking productivity app, found that:

"The 10% of employees with the highest productivity surprisingly didn't put in longer hours than anyone else. In fact, they didn't even work full eight-hour days. What they did was take regular breaks." ("The Exact Amount of Time You Should Work in a Day," *Fast Company Magazine),* 09/15/14.

In order for organizations to have a culture of innovation, employees need to be encouraged to take time to consider better approaches to the work they're doing and to the products and services they're delivering. How do employees in a guilt-ridden nation find time to consider breakthrough ideas?

The first step is to realize that most ideas don't come out of the blue when your mind is focused on the task at hand. Time should be dedicated to consider different ways of doing things by turning your mind off. This will only happen when employees have dedicated time to generate ideas to feed into the organization's innovation process.

As a starting point, employees should dedicate a few hours each week to idea generation. The work calendar should be partitioned off, and each employee will need to book the time so no distractions will interfere with idea generation. If there is calendar software available to prevent others from inviting you to a meeting, use the software to notify others that this part of your day is not available.

After dedicating a few hours each week for a few weeks, some employees will find this is more than enough time, while others may feel the need to increase the dedicated time. Adjustments should be made as necessary. Ensure your deliverables are being met, and ensure that you are dedicating necessary time to help your business thrive.

What is the best time to set aside? This will vary by staff member. Each staff member should attempt different hours of the day when starting out to find the best time for them. Adjustments should be made where necessary. Employees in customer interface roles will want to avoid the busiest times of their day, in order to avoid distractions.

The block(s) of time needed will also vary by employee. Some people find that an hour here and there is most effective, while others are more creative with two- or three-hour blocks set aside.

If an employee is looking for a reason to spend time on generating ideas, there are 85 billion reasons. When AT&T was looking for growth in 2016, they had essentially tapped out all of their own ideas. So, their plan for growth was to acquire Time Warner for $85 billion. That is a very expensive alternative to creating a culture of innovation that helps employees find time to generate ideas that can move the firm forward.

Finding Space

As organizations continue to reduce their office footprint, finding space where an employee can go for an hour or two to avoid distractions continues to become more difficult. It is imperative, though, to optimize creativity for employees by finding a space where they can spend some time undistracted to consider innovation for the greater good of their firm.

There are still a few offices with doors that close. They are ideal to avoid distractions, particularly if there is no window on the door, or if blinds may be closed to isolate the occupant. Some of my clients have created Quiet Rooms, and have scattered them throughout the office. These rooms may be used by employees in order to avoid distractions. Other clients offer libraries in their building, where employees are encouraged to work quietly with no distractions. Closed offices, quiet rooms, and libraries are excellent locations for employees to be alone with no distractions. This will allow the best environment for ideas to be generated, in order to cultivate a culture of innovation.

However, many workplaces are not ideal. They either don't have closed offices, quiet rooms, or libraries, or don't have enough resources to accommodate all the needs of their staff. Luckily, there is a plethora of alternatives that may equally provide employees with an undistracted environment in order to generate ideas. Home offices are becoming more common, as technology evolves and office costs escalate. If the office does not give enough opportunity for employees to find a space where they can avoid distractions for a certain period of time, employees should be encouraged to spend a few hours a week at home to generate ideas. If a home office is used, ensure that a space is used where distractions will be at a minimum.

Similarly, the office may be located near a public library, where employees could go to find a space that is more conducive to generating ideas than a typical office cubicle. Also, meeting rooms may be used as an alternative to quiet rooms where possible. As well, employees with closed offices may be willing to share their office space when they are at meetings or off-site.

A lack of distractions is essential for ideal generation of ideas, so finding a space without distractions is very important. Also important is what the space includes. Some people need a simple desk and chair, while others prefer a comfortable lounge chair. Some people prefer a small pad to write on, while others prefer a large whiteboard with many different-colored markers. Still others prefer a laptop or tablet, while a few people may prefer crayons. Whatever tools you deem essential for idea generation, ensure you find a space that can accommodate them.

Free the Mind

Finding time and space to generate ideas is imperative to optimizing the process of generating ideas. Once the time and space are selected, an employee is often left in an empty room with a lot of things to think about. The next step, however, is to not think about anything and to free the mind.

There is no room for filters when considering new ideas. Ideas need to flow freely, and this will only happen when the mind is first set free. A few simple steps can accomplish this.

First, close your eyes. Take a few deep breaths and count to seven. Then focus your mind on a large, empty white circle. Imagine the circle getting bigger and bigger until all you see is white.

Let Your Mind Wander

With time and space set aside, it is now time to fill the mind with thoughts. For some people, this is the easiest part. Their mind is always wandering, and thinking of different ways of doing things. For most of us, though, aids are needed to help us come up with creative ideas. This section outlines several tips and tools to aid your mind in creating new and innovative thoughts.

There are several aids that may be of assistance. They can be broken down into external stimuli, areas to consider, and recording apparatuses. Some people find listening to music can help the mind wander and veer off the path of work that is waiting outside the Quiet Room door. Some find classical music to be of most help, while others need heavy rock to get the heart pumping in order to be creative. When starting out, it is best to experiment with various genres to see which helps you the most. Remember to use headphones or earplugs if coworkers are in the immediate vicinity.

Another possible external stimulus is art. Paintings, photographs, and drawings are often open to multiple interpretations. Creativity can be stimulated by examining the minute details of what the artist or photographer has created, and by considering the impact of how the details help to create the larger picture. Similarly, creativity may be stimulated by considering what the artist's frame of mind must have been when he or she created that piece of art, or by considering why the photographer chose to take that picture at that time.

A third possible stimulus is poetry, or other types of fiction. There are many distractions, at a conscious or subconscious level, that are drawing your mental energy as you try to create new ideas. By reading poetry or other types of fiction, your mind can turn its focus to a fictional world, which is really the place where innovation currently lies. That is, any innovation would, by definition, require a change from the way things are to another way. So the new way is now fiction, since it doesn't currently exist.

Another possible stimulus for fiction is a movie or play or television show. By watching videos, which is easier now than ever with smartphones, and an entertainment world that is available 24 hours a day, people can escape the current situation they're in and start imagining another world of wonder.

The above stimuli are useful if you are restricted in where you can go. Another possibility is to get out of the office and wander outside your normal office environment. Soak up the sights and smells around you, and think about your surroundings.

With the mind free, either through external stimuli or through internal efforts, it is time to focus your thinking. Since the intent of this exercise is to come up with innovative ideas that will help your firm's business position, it is helpful to consider ideas toward that end. In an ideal world, you have been given an objective for the year, and you can focus your thoughts on alternatives to reach that objective. If this is the case, then the issue becomes one of brainstorming. See Chapter 3 for tools on how to brainstorm when the objective is known.

In many cases, the objective is not known. Employees are encouraged to generate ideas to help the business move forward, but there are, effectively, no limits. In cases such as these, there are many directions in which to go.

To move the company forward, there is incremental innovation and there is explosive innovation. Incremental innovation requires small changes to make things different. In the product arena, an example of this would be a toilet paper company making its rolls larger. In the service area, an example would be adding a warranty to assist buyer confidence.

Explosive innovation requires larger changes. It typically involves completely changing the way things are done. An example would be Google, a search engine provider, getting into self-driving cars. When considering ideas to help innovation move along in your organization, it is good to explore both incremental and explosive innovation. Incremental innovation is often easier to provide a business case for, since it's based on something that is already a known variable within the organization. Meanwhile, explosive innovation is a greater risk, since it's often venturing into new territory for your organization.

There are several directions your mind can wander in that may allow for either incremental or explosive innovation.

One direction worth exploring is the world of the contrarian. Instead of considering simple extensions (such as a cell phone company considering more features), look at things that your company would never be involved with. Try to list 10 things that your company would never do. This could involve product or service ideas, or how the company interacts with its customers. Ask yourself why your company is not involved with these things, and consider the possibility of what would happen if they were to be involved with these things.

Another possible direction is to consider cross industry success. That is, look at how a different industry has achieved success in a certain area, and consider if it's possible that its success could be duplicated in your industry. An example would be a service provider looking at the success of Netflix. Part of Netflix's success is its pricing strategy, where customers pay a monthly fee for unlimited movies. Could that pricing model be applied to other services?

A third direction to look at is the process model. Try to map out the processes within your organization. Look at how your products and services are conceived, and then selected, marketed, created, and delivered. What part of the process seems to be the most successful? Which is the least successful? Are there areas to make strong parts stronger, or do you have ideas on how to strengthen the weakest links? Consider as well if some steps can be avoided altogether.

Customer feedback can be a wealth of information for generating innovative ideas. Customers may be able and willing to tell you what expectations they have that are not being met. Similarly, they may give you suggestions on what other industries or some of your competitors are doing that you're not. Unfortunately, customer feedback can be hard to process, so some companies do not take it seriously enough. One of my clients was an educational institution that had over 75,000 students come through their doors every year, and over 150,000 students taking courses online. They kept great track of the numbered responses on their evaluation sheets, since it was easy to track and compare year over year. Unfortunately, the textual comments were much harder to track. They had one person to examine and address the comments for improvement, which was woefully insufficient. A great source for business innovation was lost!

Another direction is personal interests. What are you most passionate about? Could you generate ideas to create a more ideal working environment? Is there a possibility of better aligning your company's products and services with your personal passions? Turning new ideas into action will require a lot of work and/or persuasion, so passion is a key ingredient to have.

Also consider the way things are done now. Are they serving the business well, or causing issues? When new employees ask the veterans why things are done a certain way, the response "because it's always been done that way" is inexcusable. If something irks you about the way certain things are done at your organization, consider alternatives.

A few years ago, I interviewed Isadore Sharp, the Canadian founder of the Four Seasons hotel chain. He started with a construction business, purchased a hotel in Toronto, and turned the business into a global success story with luxury hotels in every corner of the world. While speaking with him, I asked him how he was able to come up with innovative ideas that changed the luxury hotel industry while ignoring the advice of many of the naysayers at the time.

> Opinions are expressed based on past fact. Ask yourself, "What is the future?" I like trying things that other people don't see. You see the risks. You know there will be a possible penalty to pay. As long as it's not destructive, follow your "subconscious belief"—it's a fanatical belief—that what you're doing will work.

Another consideration is form versus function. What is the function of the products and services your company is providing? The function of banking has not changed over the last 30 years, but the form has changed dramatically. If people want to pay my firm for a service, the money is still transferred from the client's bank account to the vendor's bank account. But 30 years ago, the form was predominantly checks, while today, the form is predominantly electronic. This has provided many benefits for the service provider.

Thirty years ago, I worked in the engineering department at a major bank. I was hired for four months on a work term, and I figured I might as well open an account with the bank. After two weeks, they gave me a paycheck, which was the norm back then. I went to a branch of the bank and deposited a check from that bank. Although it would probably be unheard of today, the check was held for five weeks until my identity and the check were verified!

The major banks have, for the most part, changed their form to continue to provide the same function of banking. Many businesses have refused to change their form, since they considered it part of their business. Early examples of this were the train companies. They were in the business of transporting people and goods from one place to another. Unfortunately, they saw themselves as transporting people and goods from one place to another by train. When the air travel industry came along, most train companies saw it as a threat, rather than a continuation of their services.

> *"If Thomas Edison invented electric light today, Dan Rather would report it on CBS News as, 'Candle-making industry threatened.'"*
> —Newt Gingrich

Similarly, major industry leaders have harmed themselves by sticking to the form of their business rather than its function. Blockbuster was in the business of renting videos to customers. Unfortunately, they saw themselves as being in the business of renting videos to customers at retail outlets. When they looked into renting videos online, which was the natural progression with their established customer base, some senior managers saw it as a threat to their retail outlets, so they did not want to pursue that business aggressively enough. Eventually, the function of renting videos online became so popular that Blockbuster declared bankruptcy.

Other organizations have attempted to redefine the function of what businesses do. Some have been an evolution. There was, for example, no need for search engines before the World Wide Web appeared. But as the number of websites skyrocketed, the need for search engines skyrocketed as well. Some redefinition of business functions has been an attempt to create new markets. The concept of "sharing" has redefined many industries by redefining the rules and regulations of major industries. Napster introduced the concept of wide-scale music sharing, where people could listen to music other people had purchased. Before Napster, you could go to your friend's house and listen to a CD there, but Napster allowed this sharing to be done on a massive scale. A student in Louisiana could now listen to a CD on a computer in Montana.

Uber has attempted to redefine the taxi industry by calling their service a ride-sharing program. Some municipalities have accepted the new definition, some have opposed it, and some have created rules similar to those of the taxi industry that Uber must follow.

The form of the retail industry continues to evolve, while the function continues to stay the same. The function of a retailer is to sell products to a consumer. As the Internet grew, many consumers switched to online purchasing. A benefit to the retailers is that their reach has grown. Thirty years ago, it would have been hard for many customers to find a small store in Jacksonville, Florida, that specializes in specific gadgets. Now, anyone in the world may find that store. A detriment to the retailers is that with increased reach comes increased competition.

One of the issues now with online shopping is the length of time it takes for the product to be delivered. Retailers continue to investigate alternatives. Many major retailers, including grocery stores, are offering the option for customers to purchase online and then show up at the store for pickup. A typical trip to the grocery store used to take an hour; now the grocery list can be ordered from home, and picked up in two or three minutes at express parking spots. Amazon is attempting to use drones to fly products to your house in minimal time.

As you consider possible new directions for your organization, consider the functions and the current forms that you are using. Make a list of all the functions. What is it that your business actually does? After asking the *What* questions, ask yourself *how* the products and services are provided. Is it dependent on the form? Is there a way of removing the dependency of the form? What new forms are being used in the marketplace today?

"Edison's electric light did not come from the continuous improvement of candles."

—Oren Harari

The electric light is a great example of explosive innovation that created the same function (light) as a candle, but in a much different form.

Generating new business does not always come cheap. Many of the major carriers in the United States have seen their revenues flatline when most Americans have phones and a cell phone plan. With little room to grow, the carriers have looked elsewhere for growth. Since they have witnessed their client base's need for constant entertainment, several of the large carriers have been trying to grow by buying entertainment content providers. Comcast purchased NBC. Verizon purchased Yahoo, and then AT&T offered $85 billion to acquire Time Warner. These carriers should have innovated sooner. The writing was on the wall that they were nearing their limit on the voice and data.

One Plus One Equals a Billion (Recording and Sharing Ideas)

Ideas may flow like the water in a gentle stream or like Niagara Falls. In either case, it's important that the ideas are captured for later evaluation. There are many tools available to record your ideas.

The traditional method of recording ideas is using a pen or pencil on blank paper. Whether it's a giant flip chart, or sheets of standard loose-leaf, grab your favorite writing tool (pens, crayons, colored pencils, etc.) and start drawing or writing. As computers become more prevalent, handwriting has become less popular due to the limited ability to edit and share the information. It is, however, a great way of recording your ideas and thoughts, unless your handwriting is completely illegible.

Since computers are more prevalent, you could start typing on a tablet, a laptop, or a desktop computer. This can be great for text, but is often more time-consuming for images.

There are also many alternatives. Many of my clients have Smart boards that allow one to use handwriting on a whiteboard, which then gets easily captured. Some of the handwriting may be translated into digital text, which effectively allows you to enter your thoughts as handwriting but store them as text. Many tablets also have the ability to translate handwriting into text.

Other alternatives for recording your thoughts are plentiful. Some people write their ideas on a whiteboard or flip chart, and then take a picture with their smartphone. Others may use an audio recorder, which allows them to think and speak freely, and then edit later. Still others use the video function on their smartphone to record everything—their handwriting and their spoken words.

As the need for innovation continues to grow in businesses of all sizes, there continue to be new solutions for recording and sharing ideas. A company named SoapBox has created an enterprise wide software solution to help companies record and share ideas. There is no doubt that more companies will create larger software solutions. The important thing to remember is that the software itself is no substitute for the human brain.

If you're unsure of the best method in your particular case, different methods may be selected at the beginning to help you decide. The important thing here is that you record your thoughts for later consideration and review.

There are very few people in this world, particularly at a young age, that possess the ability to look at business ideas from technical, business, and financial perspectives. So it is good to share your idea with others before presenting it to your firm so that the idea will be strengthened.

I was involved in the early years of software development, and at that time, business people were unsure of what technology could actually provide. Young software engineers like me could see the potential, and, to a certain extent, thought anything was possible. To capture this enthusiasm, business teams would let the software engineers document the business requirements, and then the business team would hand down their comments and approval. Over the years, most businesses switched to a process where there would be a business analyst as an intermediary between the business team and software development team. These business analysts could then guide the software engineers toward something that could bridge the best of both client needs and the technology at hand.

Once your ideas are recorded, you should start asking some of your peers in different departments to get together and discuss the ideas. An ideal situation would be to have someone from each of the following departments: finance, business, and operations. If your business relies heavily on customer service, then ensure someone from customer service is present. If your business relies heavily on technology, then ensure someone from the technology group is there.

Once the team is assembled, follow the same process as discussed in the above sections. Dedicate time. Find a space that would be comfortable for the entire team and where there will be no distractions. Consider the ideas you have generated, as well as ideas some of your team members have created.

It is important to note that there should be very few restrictions on what is discussed in these team reviews. For instance, a technology expert does not have to limit his or her comments to technology. Objections do not have to be avoided in order to create harmony. In fact, objections from team members are excellent to note because they will probably appear later from other staff as the idea moves down the Infectious Innovation Process funnel (see Figure 2.1).

If the team is functioning well, there may be a lot of progress in a very short time. If so, it's important to keep the team together, and perhaps switch to new ideas being generated on a team level.

There are several things that could go wrong with a team. I've seen teams where one or more members are not contributing at all. In this case, you could either excuse the noncontributing member, or advise the noncontributing member that they will be excused if they continue to lack input to the conversations. Sometimes, there can be strong yet opposing personalities in a team where each is trying to "win" the contest by getting the other members to agree with their solution. In these cases, the team should come up with a group consensus where possible. If not possible, then the team should be disbanded and reorganized to allow positive progress.

Another issue with teams discussing ideas occurs when organizations are offering incentives for innovative ideas. Team members may believe their input is more valuable than those of fellow team members, and may feel they deserve a greater slice of the incentive. In cases where there are financial incentives for these ideas, it is important for the person organizing the team to lay out the sharing of the incentive at the beginning. The incentive should always be shared equally among the team members.

This is a common issue with owners of start-up businesses. They often reach a peak where they need financing to grow. At this point, business leaders need to decide if they want a small piece of a big pie, or a big piece of a small pie.

The same situation occurs when an individual has an idea that may bring a big incentive. They have to decide if they would rather strengthen the idea by involving cross functional peers, or submit the idea to get the entire incentive. Synergy of a team will often provide a better idea submission, and then strengthen the chance of acquiring the incentive.

Once the ideas are submitted, they enter the collection phase.

Summary

Generate ideas to fill the Infectious Innovation Process funnel
Assign time to idea generation
Find the space needed to think

- Distraction-free
- Comfortable

Free your mind
Consider external stimuli when generating ideas

- Music, art, poetry, TV, movies
- Explore outdoors

Use several methods to generate business innovation ideas

- Contrarian views
- Process models
- Customer feedback
- Success in other industries

- Personal interests
- How are things done now?
- Form versus function

Record ideas so they can be collected

- Smart boards, tablets, or laptops
- Flip charts or whiteboards
- Audio or video recording

Share ideas with a cross functional team to strengthen the idea

CHAPTER 3

Idea Collection (Don't Let the Good Ones Go)

Staff members should be coming up with ideas on an ongoing basis. There is not a creative season, where ideas flourish for only a part of the year. Rather, the ideas should be flowing like water.

And the ideas are continually flowing. Human beings are creative individuals by nature. As children, we are always asking "why?" and continuously trying new things. When my son was four years old, the sun was still out, but the moon was also visible in the sky. He turned to me and asked why the moon was out during the day. I didn't really know the answer. I tried my best to explain the scientific reason for reflection of the sunrays, but by the time I had considered and delivered an answer, his mind had wandered to another curiosity. As adults, we should still seek out our curious side.

In the workforce, there is a tendency toward pushing this creativity toward a certain goal: making a widget, writing a software program, filing, and so on. But the simplest day-to-day tasks require creativity. How to get to work and how to get home can cause people to adapt. Buses can be early or late. Car accidents can occur on the road. Bike lanes can be blocked by nature. In each case, human beings need to find creative ways to adapt on a random basis.

On the job, workers get sick or leave the company. Priorities of senior management change. Nature, such as snow storms or tornados, may cause havoc on what should be a normal workday. Shipments of materials may be delayed. The human mind is often being asked to adapt and be creative at work, even in the most mundane jobs.

Early in my career, I was working at a start-up that had just sold its largest supply of fingerprint scanners to a company with its headquarters

Infectious innovation process

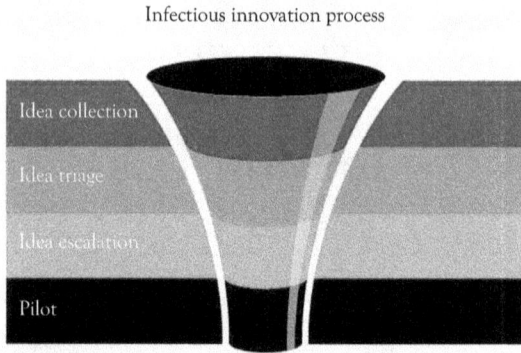

Figure 3.1 Infectious innovation process funnel

in New York. A celebration was held later that day in the office. As we were celebrating, the president got a phone call. The truck delivering the scanners veered off the road and into a water-filled ditch. Most of the scanners were rendered useless! The celebration was short-lived since no one had filed insurance on the delivery. We all adapted though.

So staff members are, for the most part, often called on for creative solutions to problems, which are sometimes random and sometimes predictable.

In Chapter 2, there were many ideas on how to turn that creativity into business innovation ideas. What happens, however, at many companies is that many employees have ideas. Some of these ideas are complex, while some are simple. Either simple or complex ideas could lead to a dramatic increase of revenues. Senior management, however, needs to know about them, or they will be lost.

In order to ensure ideas are captured, this chapter discusses how to collect the ideas, which is the top rung of our Infectious Innovation Process (see Figure 3.1).

The Twenty-First-Century Suggestion Box

In the twentieth century, employees were encouraged to submit their ideas for improving the company into a suggestion box. They would write down their idea on paper, and then place it into the suggestion box, which was often locked to help contributors to stay anonymous. That is, no one could follow them, open the box, and read their suggestion without the contributor knowing.

I have had clients that continue to have a similar suggestion box well into the twenty-first century. It is placed near the elevator or stairs so that it is clearly visible to those who wish to submit an idea. Those clients, however, are few and far between. The suggestion box has mostly been replaced by one of the following methods to collect ideas.

Electronic Collection

Every large business, and pretty well every small and medium-sized business, has collected large amounts of information on many topics, and has structures in place to store and retrieve information of many types. As a result, there are often people already involved with the company's information management. Adding a structure for ideas on business innovation is a natural progression to a business's information management structure, and selecting the people to oversee the collection is usually a straightforward process.

An electronic collection of employee ideas on business innovation has many advantages. It allows for employees from any office to contribute, regardless of the location of the employee. Another advantage is that employees can elect to contribute anonymously or with credit. Similarly, an electronic collection system allows online sharing to encourage augmentation and improvement of ideas. When two employees come up with similar ideas, an electronic collection system can time-stamp ideas, so incentives can be handed out to the original submission. Similarly, an electronic system could be upgraded to advise submitters when similar ideas have been submitted in the past, thus avoiding duplication of ideas.

Innovation Contests

Many companies hold contests where employees can submit ideas to help the company innovate. A deadline is chosen for all employees to present ideas by, and employees are advised they may submit ideas either as individuals or as teams. Sometimes, there are guidelines in place, such as minimum revenue targets.

An advantage of this type of collection mechanism is that there is often a format for submissions, which makes it easier for the competition committee to compare ideas. Another advantage is that there is no need for constant reminders to people to submit ideas. This is usually an annual event that allows people to focus for a short time, thus internal marketing of the innovation campaign is restricted in length of time.

This is particularly useful where businesses have a large base of employees who have been with the company for a long time. There is often a history of management reportedly not listening to employee ideas, so employees are not up for a continual submission of ideas. Once a year seems ideal for the ones that still want to share their ideas, no matter how jaded they have become.

A disadvantage of this collection mechanism is that lightning may strike at any time. Often, a week or two after the deadline, employees will have great ideas that have to wait for the next contest. Another disadvantage is that employees are not encouraged the rest of the year to come up with revenue-increasing innovations.

Hackathon

Having been involved with computer software since I joined the Carleton University High School Computer Science Club in 1977, I have heard hacking used in many areas of software. Predominantly there are two meanings of hacking. The first commonly accepted definition of hacking is to break into a secure environment with software. This was popularized in 1984 in the movie *War Games* where Matthew Broderick was able to break into the U.S. defense systems when he thought he had found a new video game. A second commonly accepted definition of hacking is to create inelegant, inefficient software that does the job it's intended to.

A hackathon is based on the second definition, namely creating an inelegant and inefficient software solution. Hackathons in businesses can last anywhere from a day to a week. The intention of a hackathon is to gather a group of software development staff (which may include coders, project managers, product managers, etc.) to create a quick and dirty solution that can lead to business innovation for the company. Similar to a jam session among musicians, different staff members will throw out ideas, and coders will try to create quick, often inelegant, solutions to see what's possible.

As different ideas are discussed and experimented with, business innovation may occur. An advantage of this method to collect ideas is that there are many collaborators together at once to add synergy to the discussion. Another advantage is that it often results in a working, although preliminary, prototype.

A disadvantage of this method for idea collection is that it is more costly for non-software companies. This, however, can be quite effective if a non-software company is committed to the prototyping of a new product in a short period of time, and will invest the money in various resources. An example would be a beverage company that is looking for new product ideas. If they invest in a wide arrangement of possible ingredients, and in a large assortment of different packaging ideas, they could "hack" out a new product idea in a short period of time.

Innovation Brainstorming Sessions

Some companies like to gather various subsets of employees every so often to sit down and generate new product and service ideas for the company. A facilitator will be chosen to help the assembled staff to generate and document their ideas. The ideas may be recorded on handwritten sheets, a computer, a Smart board or a recording device (video or audio). When this is a company's strategy to collect ideas for business innovation, there are normally several subsets of staff gathered, and all the ideas are collected and entered into an information management structure that may or may not be accessible to all employees.

An advantage of this technique is that everyone, in theory, has the right to speak up and present their idea. It is especially useful if employees have individually gone through the steps in Chapter 2 first. There is often a synergy that occurs when one person presents an idea, and others are encouraged to add on to it.

A disadvantage of this technique may be team dynamics. Although everyone is encouraged to speak, outgoing people may take much of the discussion, whereas a creative person in the corner may not want to present an idea in a group setting. The person may fear their idea is not good enough or worth considering in a group setting, but would otherwise contribute to an electronic bulletin board.

Another disadvantage of this technique is that this often occurs no more than once a year.

Employees may come up with dramatic revenue-improvement business innovation ideas at any time. If employees are following the steps suggested in Chapter 2, they will be exercising their business innovation creativity muscles on a weekly basis. So an electronic collection of ideas should always be available to capture these ideas. In order to enhance the electronic collection of ideas, the last three collection methods (innovation contests, hackathons, and innovation meetings) should be added to the mix to improve the ideas.

Incentives

Incentives are not compulsory in order to collect employee ideas. Many employees will gladly offer their ideas and will have no problem sharing them with colleagues. Most organizations believe that management, in particular, should be continually looking to raise the bar within the company. As a result, they should be continually submitting ideas for growth.

If ideas are being collected through brainstorming sessions, it is rare that people expect a prize or reward for contributing ideas. With an innovation contest, however, expectations are much higher for some sort of prize.

Financial Incentives

Financial incentives may be offered in a number of ways. There could be a fixed or variable award made to the person or people who contributed to an idea that is followed and has an effect on the bottom line. A decision should be made and publicized on what happens when more than one person submits the same profitable idea. Will the first person to submit the idea be awarded the incentive? Will anyone who submitted the idea be awarded the incentive? Or will the incentive be shared among all contributors with the same idea?

For example, if an incentive of $1,000 is given to all ideas that make it to the revenue-generating or cost-cutting phase and, let's say, four people submitted the same idea, then, either the first person to submit it wins $1,000 or all four of them win $1,000 each. Or the $1,000 is split among the four, and each submitter would receive $250.

The size of the incentive may be fixed or variable. There could be a decision to give out a fixed amount no matter what the size of the innovation. Or, there could be an increasing scale of incentive based on the effect of the innovation.

The downside of financial incentives is that there may be less sharing of ideas. That is, if an employee feels they have a good idea, and there is an incentive on the line, they may be less inclined to discuss the idea with others before submitting the idea. This lack of sharing may cause dilution of the idea.

I ventured on my own in 2001. At the time, I met with many other local entrepreneurs and would discuss investors. Some of the "vulture capitalists," as they were called by less respectful entrepreneurs, would only invest in a young company if they could get a large percentage of the company. Some entrepreneurs were very skeptical, while others encouraged the investment. A typical question asked in entrepreneur circles is, "Would you rather own 100 percent of a million dollar company, or 20 percent of a billion dollar company?"

While many entrepreneurs appreciate outside investment for growth, internal idea contributors should be shown the value of sharing their idea to strengthen its value. Would they rather win 50 percent of the incentive for a strong idea, or 100 percent of no incentive for a not-as-strong idea?

Nonfinancial Incentives

Over the years, my clients have offered numerous nonfinancial incentives for superior performance. These ideas could be used as well as financial incentives for innovative ideas that have an effect on the bottom line of the company.

One of my clients reserved parking spots close to the building for special occasions. Several of my clients recognize outstanding performers at department assemblies or all-staff meetings. Other clients recognize outstanding performers in a company newsletter. One company I worked at early in my career gave out necklaces with carrots on them for all team members on projects that were successful. On the first day of each month, everyone with carrots would parade around the office with all the carrots they had accumulated over the years. Any of these incentives could be used as incentives for winners of innovation contests, or for employees who had submitted ideas that turned into profit-increasing products, services, or processes.

Raising Hope

As innovation becomes more a piece of the fabric of many successful organizations, there are more and more opportunities for employees to submit ideas on innovation. With increasing amounts of opportunity, there may be increasing frustration for many employees that their fantastic ideas are not being heard.

The success of the Infectious Innovation Process depends on ideas continually being contributed. This will not happen if all employees feel jaded rather than hopeful.

Some business leaders are more passionate about hope than others. Frank O'Dea is a serial entrepreneur who has founded several successful organizations in different industries. When you see premium coffee shops on every major street corner, it's hard to believe there was ever a time when premium coffee shops were few and far between. In 1975, however, there was no premium coffee industry in Canada, until Frank O'Dea created one with his chain of Second Cup stores.

After creating an industry that became successful internationally (with stores in 13 countries), Frank then created an international paper shredding industry with his second successful business, Proshred.

When I interviewed Frank for a blog with *Fast Company* magazine, he mentioned that the success of any organization comes down to hope, vision, and action. He felt it is absolutely imperative that staff members at all levels of an organization have hope in the company's future, and that all staff members are aware of and embrace the organization's vision statement. Action will then follow if success is to be had.

Hope alone doesn't fill the suggestion box. If the number of ideas being submitted is dwindling, an organization might want to consider switching up idea collection mechanisms. Nothing gets the creative juices flowing more than a little change in routine.

If the twenty-first-century suggestion box is drying up, gather cross functional teams for some innovation brainstorming sessions. Or hold an innovation contest to limit the time that people are expected to think about ideas for new products, services, or processes. It's also possible to use different schemes with different divisions or locations. Have the Chicago office run an innovation contest while the New York office has innovation brainstorming sessions. If different techniques are being used throughout the organization, then the ideas should be recorded with the source. Did it come from a suggestion box, innovation contest, brainstorming session, or a hackathon? By collecting this information with the ideas, an organization can determine if some collection mechanisms are more, or less, successful than other mechanisms.

Remote and Colocated Offices

Many employees these days work from home offices or work in departments that are located in several cities and/or countries. Collecting ideas from such work environments presents its own problems.

Technology exists to help the collection of ideas from every location in the world, but it does not necessarily enable the collection of ideas if staff are unfamiliar with or unaware of it.

Electronic Collection

This is probably the most straightforward mechanism to collect ideas from remote and colocated offices. An e-mail is typically sent out that lets employees know the process for submitting ideas. Remote and colocated staff usually have access to digital repositories, but this needs to be verified. When ideas are generated, the remote and colocated staff submit their ideas to the digital repository.

Innovation Contest

This is also a fairly straightforward method to collect ideas from employees working in remote and colocated offices. Rules of the contest are usually sent out, and they will tell the employees how and where to submit their ideas online. As long as the remote and colocated staff have access to the necessary repositories, ideas may be submitted to the aforementioned repository when generated.

Hackathon

This collection method can work for hackathons of software solutions, but the organization's technology needs to be more advanced. Instead of just submitting ideas, remote and colocated employees will have to be able to work with ideas in progress as software is created and modified in real time. Two-way communication is needed, and audio-visual feeds are recommended to see what is happening at headquarters while the hackathon is in progress.

If the hackathon is intended to create prototypes for hardware solutions or other tangible goods, such as beverages, it is extremely hard to include remote and colocated workers. The organization is much better off having all employees in the same boardroom or lab to hack out a new innovation.

Innovation Brainstorming Session

This collection mechanism can work for remote and colocated employees, but it will not be as effective if the employees are not all in the same location. There can either be an audio-visual feed connecting the participants, or there can be textual software that allows anyone to type into the conversation. In the case of an audio-visual feed, there needs to be a master of ceremonies who directs the conversation coming from multiple locations. The video feed should be fixed on the main boardroom where the brainstorming session is taking place, so everyone can see the list of ideas as they are contributed.

In the case of a textual software solution, all employees can connect to one piece of software in a central location. Employees communicate purely through the written word. The conversation consists of people typing in their sentences. All participants can see everything that is typed in. Usually there is a moderator collecting the ideas, and the moderator will direct the conversation as needed. An advantage of this solution is that the textual software allows all participants to download the entire conversation once complete.

Relevance is the New Black

Innovations that capture emotion may remain popular for a long time.

My first trip to Walt Disney World in Orlando, Florida, was in 1975 when the World was much smaller, and so was I. There was a Magic Kingdom with a huge castle and clean streets. My parents purchased a variety of tickets with different values, A to E. A trip on the stagecoach was considered an A ticket, while a trip on a thrill ride like Space Mountain required an E ticket.

When I went back in 1982 as a university student, the World had grown to two theme parks. The adventure was no longer a single-day event as there was too much to do.

By the time my son was born, the World had grown to four theme parks. Instead of buying tickets of different value, there was a general admission fee that would get you on all rides.

I went back in 2017 when my son was working there, and I was surprised to see some of the same rides that were there in 1975: the Dumbo ride, the Haunted Mansion, It's a Small World, Pirates of the Caribbean, Space Mountain, and several more rides continue to entertain children of all ages.

If innovations connect with people's emotions, then they can endure for 40 plus years.

In addition to tapping into customers' emotions, Disney has been able to package its value in different ways. The Pirates of the Caribbean ride had been quite popular when the movie *Pirates of the Caribbean: Curse of the Black Pearl* was filmed. The success of the movie created more demand for people to go on the ride. So the innovations of the ride and the movie worked together to exponentially multiply the interest in both the movie and the theme park attraction.

In a similar vein, visitors to the Hollywood Studios are entertained by stars of Disney Junior television shows. This causes many families to investigate Disney Junior television shows when they return from their vacation. Similarly, the success of these shows creates more demand for families to visit Hollywood Studios.

Disney has been able to find cross functional methods of developing new products and services that feed off current products and services. They have proven that in the world of innovation, relevance is the new black.

With regard to relevance and the movie business, many business people were probably surprised to see Jeff Bezos, the CEO and founder of Amazon, at the Oscars in February 2017. Amazon rose to fame as an online retailer of all things, including movies. Along the way, Amazon recognized the movie industry had changed with the advent of the Internet, and previous antitrust laws were no longer relevant.

In the mid-twentieth century, there were three major components of the movie industry: content provider, distributors, and exhibitors. Movies would be produced by the content provider, distributed by a movie distributor, and then exhibited in a movie theater. The big five studios at the time saw the benefit of controlling all three links in the chain. They could control the movies they were distributing and they could control which movies were being exhibited in their theaters. The big studios loved the arrangement, but the U.S. government and small studios felt it was not fair.

In 1948, the Supreme Court ruled against the big five studios and told them they could no longer own movie theaters. This opened up competition in the movie industry, and allowed smaller studios a chance at having their movies seen.

When the Internet came along, the content provider, distributor, and exhibitor chain became less distinctive. There were lots of people producing movies, but the Internet allowed websites to exhibit the movies without a distributor. To further fog the field, the television industry worked in a different manner. Large networks would typically be the content provider and would show network-produced movies exclusively on their own network. Cable channels such as the Home Box Office (HBO) were producing and exhibiting their own movies and television shows.

Hence, with the Internet, online retailers became exhibitors with video streaming services. The problem for regulators was that the Hollywood

Antitrust Case of 1948 prohibited content providers from being exhibitors, while television content providers were also exhibitors. Should video streaming follow movie rules or television rules?

As online video rentals became mainstream with Netflix, there was soon a comparison between Netflix and HBO. Who had more subscribers? Who had more revenues? In the business world, the online video rental providers were seen more as television exhibitors than movie exhibitors.

This opened the path for other content providers to become exhibitors. Netflix started producing its own content and showing it to subscribers. The model was successful globally, and other competitors got into the market, which brings us to Amazon.

Amazon started a video streaming service, and then decided to also become a content provider and distributor. It distributed *Manchester by the Sea*, starring Casey Affleck, and an Iranian thriller, *The Salesman*, both of which won Academy Awards in 2017. This made Amazon the first video streaming service to win an Oscar. In 2016, it picked up several Emmys for its television series *Transparent*.

Are there areas for new products and services in your organization that are relevant to current products and services your organization is offering to its customers? Can you think of ways to stimulate more interest in current products by adding relevant products and services?

Not many organizations are in the theme park and movie business, but many organizations may use this technique to grow. Consider your organization's main strengths, and then dream up new products and services to feed off these strengths.

Take out a piece of loose leaf paper and make a list of your company's strengths. For each strength, add two or three possible relevant products and services that may appear. Add these thoughts to your collection mechanism.

Open Collection Mechanisms

There are many examples of modern idea generation and collection mechanisms that are used for purposes beyond one organization's desire to create new products and services. Hackathons, in particular, are being used to allow software designers to express their creativity, often for a specific purpose.

There is an event called "Music Hack Day" that brings together those interested in innovating software and hardware involved in music productions. It has been held nine times since 2009. Similarly, there are "Science Hack Days," "Legal Tech Hack Days," "Health Tech Hack Days," and many other hack days dedicated to specific purposes. The number continues to grow.

These hack days are usually dedicated to a collection of software engineers who want to use their creativity to see where it will take them. They are grouped with other interested parties, such as practitioners (e.g., musicians) and policy makers where applicable.

As I am writing this, a local Hacking Health event is taking place that brings together software engineers, health care practitioners, and policy makers in an effort to create health technology innovations.

How can these open hack days help your organization? There are several ways. Because it brings together different members of a specific community, a hack day allows your software developers to hear real-world problems and meet policy makers in a somewhat informal setting. Second, it allows your staff to find out what other innovations are being looked into. This can be used to feed ideas into your own Infectious Innovation Process funnel. Third, it allows your organization to collect ideas from other creative individuals who may have great ideas but no mechanism to turn those ideas into new products or services.

The downside of all these hack days is that they are usually held during off-work hours, so getting people to attend may be a challenge.

Summary

Twenty-first-century Suggestion Box

- Electronic collection
- Innovation contests
- Hackathon
- Innovation brainstorming sessions

Incentives

- Financial incentives
- Nonfinancial incentives

Raising Hope

- Hope is essential for innovation
- When hope fades, mix things up

Remote and Colocated offices

- Electronic collection and innovation contests are easiest

Relevance is the New Black

- Look for relevance between current offerings and new innovation

Open Collection Mechanisms

- External events for the good of an industry or common interest
- Possibly helpful to meet interested parties and gather idea

CHAPTER 4

Filtering Ideas (Most Bang for the Buck)

In a large organization, there can be a large number of ideas resulting from different collection mechanisms (be it contests, brainstorming, or twenty-first-century suggestion boxes). At large organizations, an innovation contest with a month-long entry window can result in hundreds, if not thousands, of ideas for increasing profits. Similarly, enterprisewide brainstorming sessions result in a large amount of ideas collected.

Some of the ideas may be good ideas. In fact, some can be billion dollar ideas. But the timing needs to be right, as well as the client environment. Early in my career, I was at a new product brainstorming session and there were plenty of good ideas brought forward.

I was working with a telecommunications firm, and one of the contributors was an avid fisherman. He had lots of great ideas to make better fish-finders, but there wasn't much of an appetite to move forward with any of them since the company was a B2B company, and the fish-finders were meant for a B2C market.

Another idea that arose that day was a video on demand type service. It was the early '90s, and there was no real Internet at that point. Cable companies, however, were showing movies on certain channels, but wanted a piece of the video rental market. People who wanted to rent videos at that point had to go to their local video store and choose a VHS copy of the video they wanted to rent. Since it seemed like a good match between consumers who didn't want to leave their house to rent videos and cable companies who wanted to add the video rental service to their portfolio, a skunk works type project began to investigate the possibility for the technology that would later be called video streaming.

The video streaming project grew legs and became a piece of the product manager's fabric. In time, however, the company was purchased for its avionics technology, and left the telecommunications and video streaming departments behind. Each of these departments became separate companies. The video streaming company was unable to compete on its own, while the telecommunications company lasted as long as its support agreements did.

This chapter discusses the various components of the triage stage. It discusses grouping, filtering, and tools to rate ideas and ends with details on business strategy. The inputs for this phase are the ideas collected from the collection phase, whether through a suggestion box, a brainstorming session, a hackathon, or an innovation contest.

The output of this phase is a reduced number of ideas that have been triaged and rated against a number of criteria. This reduced number of triaged ideas can then simplify the escalation stage, as discussed in Chapter 5.

Grouping

Hindsight is 20/20. The fish-finder and video streaming scenarios above look like the obvious decisions 25 years later. At the time, though, it seemed risky to move toward a video rental system when the organization had no experience in video technology. In your current position, with hundreds, or even thousands, of employee ideas to consider, how can you find the diamonds in the rough?

Infectious innovation process

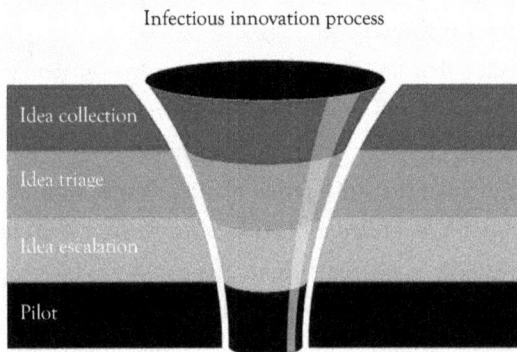

Idea collection

Idea triage

Idea escalation

Pilot

The second phase of transforming employee ideas into dramatic profits is the idea triage stage, as shown in the Infectious Innovation Process Funnel.

When ideas are coming from many sources, such as enterprisewide innovation contests or concurrent brainstorming sessions, there are undoubtedly many similar themes and maybe identical ideas. The idea triage stage allows the organization to group and prioritize the ideas that have been collected.

The first step in the triage phase is to bring down the ideas submitted to a reasonable number before an in-depth analysis can occur. Duplicate ideas should be filtered out. A well-run innovation system will have a database of previously submitted ideas as well, so duplicates of previous ideas should be filtered out. Although we are removing the duplicates from the active stream, a record of the idea should be stored as necessary. Similarly, ideas that are outside the organization's normal boundaries should be eliminated. This may include ideas that involve criminal activity. Some of my clients are divisions of larger organizations, and their boundary ends where other divisions of the organization already offer the product or service being suggested.

A quicker method to determine duplicates is to first group ideas based on similarities. For instance, you could group the ideas that involve a specific feature enhancement. An example would be a cell phone manufacturer collecting several ideas around various product features. Ideas could be grouped into: microphone, camera, speaker, settings, battery, response time, outer shell, size, and so on.

This process may be accelerated by having employees pregroup the ideas when they submit them. This will reduce the effort of grouping after submission.

Filtering

Once efforts have been made to cull duplicates and boundary breakers, an idea analysis should be done so that management can prioritize based on certain criteria. Criteria will be specific to an organization.

The first key to filtering all the ideas is to rate them against a series of criteria. There are many criteria outlined here. Each idea should be rated against each of the criteria. The criteria listed here are not an exhaustive list, and additional criteria can be added that are specific to the organization.

The criteria to be measured against are as follows:

- Relevance to current offerings
- Effect on profit
- Size of change
- Speed of launch
- Customer demand
- Costs of entering the market
- Competition
- Departments affected
- Organization-specific criteria

Relevance to Current Offerings

The bigger the ship, the harder it is to change its direction. So, it's always a good idea to look at what direction the business is currently following. Google/Alphabet has put in its list of innovation strategies to follow the 70/20/10 rule. Its goal is to have 70 percent of its innovation efforts put toward business ideas that aid its current set of product and service offerings. Twenty percent of its innovation efforts are put aside for product and service offerings that are related to its current offerings, while 10 percent of its efforts are targeted to products and services that are outside its current offerings. In some circles, this last 10 percent may be called a "moon shot." This is a good strategy to follow because it helps mitigate risks while allowing the organization to move forward on many fronts.

It is also easier for shareholders to follow the organization's strategy if most of its innovation efforts (70 percent) are being focused on current products and services.

Effect on Profit

Another grouping an organization can use to filter employee idea contributions is to look at the effect on profit. What effect will the new idea have on revenues? Small, medium, or large? Or will it have an effect on reducing costs, and, if so, how big an effect is expected? The definition of small, medium, or large is relative, and may be different for each organization. It can be either a percentage or a fixed number, for example 30 percent or $250,000.

Size of Change

A possible determining factor on whether to move forward with the idea or not is the size of the change. Are there large changes anticipated? For instance, will a brand-new sales and marketing team be needed to address a new consumer segment? Or are the changes more of a medium or small nature? Each of these terms is relative to the size of the organization making the change. When this factor is combined with the effect on profit, the filtering decision can be made much easier. If, for example, the size of the change is large, while the effect on profit is small, it's probably not the optimum idea to move forward with. However, if the size of the change is small, while the effect on the profit is large, good things can happen.

Speed of Launch

Some innovations can take a fairly long time to launch. For instance, autonomous vehicles have so many legal and insurance obstacles to overcome, that their future is still many years away. Other innovations can be done fairly quickly. For instance, changing a customer service process may be straightforward enough to be done within six months. Speed of launch can be a contributing factor to prioritizing ideas. The speed should be broken down into quick, medium-term, and long-term launches. The time frame for each factor would depend on the size of the organization. Typically a quick launch would be in the nine- to twelve-month range, while a medium-speed launch would be in the one- to two-year time frame, and a long-term launch would be more than two years.

Customer Demand

Another factor when prioritizing new ideas is customer demand. Is there any proof that customers are in search of this new innovation? Explosive innovations are often something the customer needs without the customer knowing that they need it. For example, when Uber came along with their ride-sharing service, most customers were quite familiar with the cost of taxis and the regulations that the industry had invoked to protect consumers. While customers may have had a demand for less expensive taxi service, the paradigm had not shifted away from taxis when Uber came on the scene.

So customer demand may be a hard thing to judge. It should, however, be factored into the equation when prioritizing new innovations, especially if customer feedback has indicated that this innovation will address something that customers desire.

Every organization has a customer feedback mechanism, which can be used to gauge the demand for certain innovations. When I consulted for an educational institution for public servants, there was considerable feedback regarding some of the service issues. Any innovative ideas put forward to address those issues were given first priority.

Costs of Entering the New Market

Some organizations look for innovations that have a high barrier to entry, since that will keep out the upstarts and bootstrapped companies. Are patents required? Are the costs high to enter the market? If the costs to enter the market are high, larger organizations have a better opportunity to capitalize than small companies without the disposable funding.

Meanwhile, other organizations consider it advantageous to consider innovative ideas with low up-front costs to enter the market and determine viability of the new products and services.

The levels of rating the costs of entering the market will depend on the size of the organization doing the rating, and the desire of the organization to move into new markets. Whatever the dollar values are, the costs should be rated as small, medium, or large. For example, a small cost may be under 2 percent of revenue. Medium costs may be 2 to 5 percent of revenue, and large costs may be over 5 percent of revenue. At this point, the costs are only estimates for the most part. A more accurate costing will be done in the escalation phase.

Competition

The amount of competition in the market for the new idea may be stiff, slight, or nonexistent. At this point, the rating is only an estimate. Competition may seem nonexistent until further research is conducted, especially if it's an area outside the organization's current focus.

Last year I purchased a new car and loved the unique color of that model. I thought I would easily identify my car in any crowded parking lot. After purchasing the car, I realized the color was not as unique to that model as I originally thought. Driving home one night, I saw five identical models with the same color!

Departments Affected

Some organizations choose to rate new product or service ideas based on the number of departments affected. Silos still exist, and getting interdepartmental cooperation is much harder for some companies than others. If this is a possible issue at your organization, list this as one of the criteria, and rate this as small, medium, or large. Small can indicate self-contained changes are required, while large can indicate many departments are affected, and medium is somewhere in between.

Speaking of silos, some of my clients have not been able to move forward with major initiatives because of the silos. One client had been formed by an amalgamation of provincial organizations with a common purpose. While there was a leader to unite the country, there were also leaders in each of the provincial departments, some leaders being stronger than others. Along with strong leaders in each province, some provinces felt superior to others because of their size. When major initiatives were attempted for the entire country, there were often slowdowns or blockages brought forward by the silos created. This was a major detractor for innovation here.

Another client was much smaller, but the silos were just as strong and as hard to work through. It was an educational institution with separate departments for operations, education, finance, and IT. When there was a companywide initiative to centralize and automate the collection of data from all systems for reporting purposes, each department had its own objectives and would not compromise for the common good. Working together didn't work. Leadership tried many things to move the initiative forward but only achieved success when one department was put in charge.

Organization-Specific Criteria

Every organization has additional criteria that they may choose to use to rate the ideas submitted. These criteria may be location specific, industry specific, regulatory affairs related, or based on a number of other issues. Ideally, an organization is committed to going through the process of transforming employee ideas into profit-generating returns, and learns over time which criteria have the greatest impact on the success of the transformation within the organization.

Prefiltering upon Submission

Aside from grouping, a good idea to accelerate the filtering is to have employees prefilter the ideas when they submit them. This will reduce the effort of filtering after submission. It becomes less a matter of rating the criteria, and more a matter of verifying the submitted ratings. The downside of having the submitters do the prefiltering is that the ratings may be inconsistent. Some submitters may interpret the criteria quite differently than others.

Rating the Ideas

To prepare for a more thorough analysis of idea submissions, the remaining ideas that survive the triage stage should have a rating system in place against the major criteria. Then, the decision makers will have an easier time deciding which ideas should move into the business case and/or pilot phase.

Depending on the tools at hand, there should be a table or spreadsheet that lists the various ideas against the criteria mentioned previously. A possible table created for a cell phone company might look something like this:

#	Idea	Relevance	Effect	Size	Speed	Demand	Costs	Competition	Departments
1	128MB pixel camera	L	S	S	M	S	S	Slight	S
2	Waterproof shell	L	M	S	M	S	M	Slight	M
3	Free delivery	L	S	S	S	S	S	Stiff	S
...									

Research done on each idea would depend on the number of ideas submitted, and the number of staff dedicated to the Infectious Innovation Process triage stage. The more accurate the information, the better. However, since most organizations have limited funds available to perform the triage, this rating is only intended to be an estimation exercise.

Once the table is complete, weighting could be added to the equation. For instance, if each of the eight categories were to be given equal weighting, then each criterion would be worth 12.5 percent. However, your organization may consider customer demand and speed of launch to be extremely important while costs and relevance may be less important. In this case, customer demand and speed could be given a weighting of 20 percent each, while costs and relevance would be given a weighting of 5 percent each.

This would then make the above table become as shown on page 59.

The next step would be to convert the ratings (small, medium, large, nonexistent, slight, stiff) into numerical values (1, 2, 3). The value of 3 would equate to the most desired rating, 2 to the next most desired rating, and 1 to the least desired rating. This does not always correspond to the same rating. For instance, when Relevance = Large, large would be considered a 3. However, when Costs = Large, large would be considered a 1.

Further translating the values in the chart above to numerical values, and then taking the weighting into account, a scoring system can be used to come up with a total score for each new idea, as shown on page 60.

This leaves scores of the three submitted ideas between 1.975 and 2.1, which could then be used as a general guideline to present to senior management in the escalation phase.

While this scoring mechanism can be used as a general guideline to decide which ideas should be escalated, all the scored ideas should be presented to senior management. When senior managers consider different ideas, they may have a particular affinity for one area of interest over another, which is not apparent when the scoring is performed.

A client I worked with recently on an application portfolio management project was using a similar scoring mechanism to determine which applications were worth investing in and which should be eliminated. No matter how the weighting and ratings were positioned, one senior

#	Idea	Relevance	Effect	Size	Speed	Demand	Costs	Competition	Departments
	Weighting	.05	.125	.125	.2	.2	.05	.125	.125
1	128MB pixel camera	L	S	S	M	S	S	Slight	S
2	Waterproof shell	L	M	S	M	S	M	Slight	M
3	Free delivery	L	S	S	S	S	S	Stiff	S
…									

#	Idea	Relevance	Effect	Size	Speed	Demand	Costs	Competition	Departments	Score
	Weighting	.05	.125	.125	.2	.2	.05	.125	.125	
1	128MB pixel camera	L=3	S=1	S=3	M=2	S=1	S=3	Slight =2	S=3	2.025
2	Waterproof shell	L=3	M=2	S=3	M=2	S=1	M=2	Slight =2	M=2	1.975
3	Free delivery	L=3	S=1	S=3	S=3	S=1	S=3	Stiff=1	S=3	2.1
...										

manager's pet applications always ended up in the elimination bucket. He refused to accept the scoring, and would not eliminate the application despite its weak score.

The lack of senior management support for the scoring system of innovation ideas runs a similar risk. Since senior management support is so important, as will be shown in Chapter 5, all ideas should be presented, with recommendations for what might be considered the best based on the scoring system.

Some senior managers may choose to only focus on two or three variables mentioned, while others may want more variables to be considered. So present them all.

Business Strategy

A question that often comes up when first requesting new ideas for products and services, whether through an innovation contest or hackathon or brainstorming session or suggestion box, is how much guidance should be given to the contributors. That is, should the ideas being submitted have a specific objective in mind? For example, should a cell phone manufacturing company state something to the effect of, "We are attempting to corner the market on senior citizens. Please submit all ideas and show how they can be used to help us corner the market on senior citizens"? The quick answer is No, not usually.

While every business has a strategy, and it's fantastic when new ideas are perfectly aligned with the strategy the organization is following, most companies ask for innovative ideas to expand their current strategy, and to look for future growth. Asking employees to focus their creativity in a certain area can be counterproductive. It limits the organization's growth while possibly stifling the employees' creativity.

The business strategy should be known, however, and ideas collected from employees should not immediately change the strategy. How does an organization come up with its strategy?

Whenever I've worked with business leaders on strategy, I've always emphasized the importance of keeping it simple. The ship is in motion, and there are normally just slight variations to make on an annual basis. While some organizations like to combine strategic planning with celebrations of the previous year's victories and a team-building exercise, the selection of a new strategy should be fairly straightforward.

One of the tools I like to use is from one of my mentors, Alan Weiss. He uses this straightforward approach in his consulting work to help organizations select a strategy that is easy for everyone to understand while facilitating the ability to turn strategy into tactics.

The chart below shows a cross between products, services, and relationships and competitive, superior, and breakthrough.

	Competitive	Superior	Breakthrough
Products			
Services			
Relationships			

From *Process Consulting*, page 134, Alan Weiss, 2002

During a strategic planning activity, I will ask my clients to first indicate where they are now with respect to the above table. The definition of the various terms on the left (products, services, relationships) will vary depending on industry. Companies offering financial services, for example, rarely have physical products. However, they do recognize the difference between an actual mortgage and a customer service process to help you apply and fill out the mortgage. Similarly, the difference between service and relationship may require definition. Using the earlier example of a cell phone manufacturer, the product would be the cell phone itself. A service would be a cell phone app the manufacturer may provide, such as mapping or music. The relationship would consist of how a customer would buy and use the cell phone, along with any customer service required following the use of the phone.

Warranties are an example of the difference in relationship for various cell phone providers. When my son's BlackBerry required repair due to a defect several years ago, it was shipped to a BlackBerry repair center, repaired, and then returned. They gave him a loaner but he was without his own phone for two weeks. When he later owned an iPhone and brought it in for repairs (my son is tough on his phones), they immediately gave him a replacement.

The different categories across the top represent how the organization is seen in the marketplace. Competitive indicates that the organization is no better and no worse than the majority of its competition. Superior indicates that the organization is superior to the majority of its competition, while Breakthrough indicates that the organization is vastly superior to the majority of its competition. As time goes by, the ratings degrade from right to left as the competition catches up. That is, a product seen as a breakthrough this year will probably be seen as superior or competitive in the years to come as competitors catch up.

Once the organization has indicated on the chart where they are today, they are then asked to indicate where they want to be a year or two from now. If a company is looking for explosive innovation, then it is typically looking to have breakthrough products or services. On the other end of the spectrum, an organization may be looking for incremental innovation just to remain competitive.

After the organization has selected which strategy to follow, the gap between where they are now and where they want to be must be bridged. That's where the tactics need to come into play, and accountability has to be delivered.

A business strategy is important for the forward movement of the company, and it is important for the cohesiveness of effort being applied in the various departments. But how does the Infectious Innovation Process affect the business strategy?

There is a possible relationship between the Infectious Innovation Process and the business strategy in several ways. Either the innovation ideas can help guide the strategic planning, or the strategic planning can impact the innovation ideas. If the ideas are reviewed before the strategic planning session, some ideas for ways forward can be presented at the session. Similarly, the strategy selected may impact which innovation ideas are selected to act upon, and which may be ignored for the near future.

Summary

Grouping

- Group by feature or product line
- Remove duplicates
- Remove previously entered duplicate ideas

Filtering

- Select filtering criteria

Rating

- Chart rating criteria for each idea
- Select weighting
- Determine estimated scoring of ideas

Business Strategy

- Keep the strategy simple
- Determine where you are and where you want to be
- Innovation can lead strategy or strategy can lead innovation

CHAPTER 5

Escalating Ideas (Making the Most of It)

After going through the triage stage, ideas then enter the escalation stage. Many ideas will enter here, but only a few will continue to the pilot stage. In order to survive the escalation stage, there are several steps. Senior management has to endorse the idea. Then a business case has to be made. This is followed by team selection to dig further into the details of how the proposed ideas will be handled by the organization. The stage ends by identifying business, technical, and financial issues.

Infectious innovation process

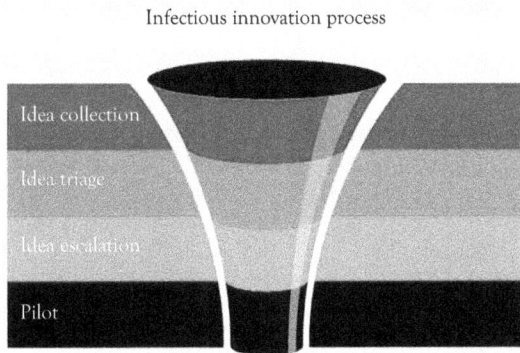

The idea escalation stage is important because it dramatically reduces the number of innovations that will make it to the pilot stage. It is often a hard step because there are so many good ideas, but it is essential not to spread the organization's resources too thin.

The input to the idea escalation stage is a number of grouped ideas that have extensive ratings for comparison. The output from the escalation stage is a number of business cases outlining possible options on the ideas selected by a specific member of senior management.

Senior Management

The larger the project, the more departments in an organization are involved. Even in this day and age, when communication technology is better than ever, there are versions of silos in every organization. In order to make interdepartmental efforts as smooth as possible, it is imperative to have the involvement of senior management. Looking at the Venn diagram in Figure 5.1 shows the importance of senior management support in innovation leadership.

Key Ingredients to Successful Innovation Leadership

As shown in the diagram, there are three key ingredients to having successful innovation leadership: strong support from senior management, high number of ideas from employees, and a strong innovation process in place. If any of these is missing, then the full impact of any item present is not realized.

Looking at the Venn diagram below, the ideal position an organization can be in is the area marked 4. This indicates that all three key ingredients are present. The other numbered areas (1, 2, 3) indicate that two of the key ingredients are present. These three areas lead to less than optimum results, as follows.

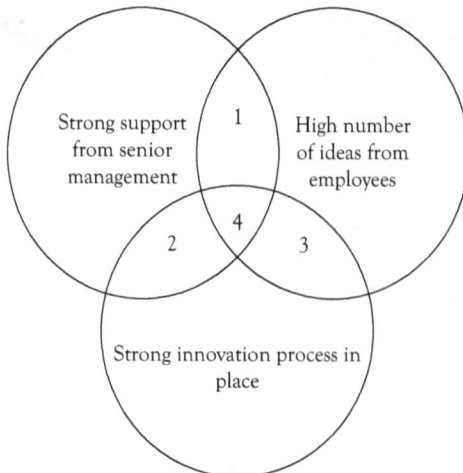

Figure 5.1 Key ingredients to successful innovation leadership

Area 1—Spinning Your Wheels

In this case, there are lots of good ideas, and senior management has shown strong support to move these ideas forward. Without a strong innovation process in place, though, the ideas will never be turned into new products or services.

Area 2—Empty Funnel

Senior management is looking for ideas and there's a good process to turn them into new products or services. But having no ideas is like having a car engine with no gas. It should be pointed out that staff members never have a lack of ideas. Rather, they are hesitant to bring ideas forward, or the idea collection system is not storing the ideas properly.

Area 3—Wasted Energy

In this scenario, there are lots of good ideas, and there's a strong process in place to turn them into new products and services. But with no senior management support in place, efforts to transform the ideas into new products and services will go nowhere.

The process is outlined in detail in this book. As long as there are lots of ideas being submitted by employees, there needs to be senior management support to keep the innovation happening.

To be clear, senior management does not have to jump on every great idea it sees. In fact, less is more. If each quarter, one member of senior management were to support one idea, there would be four new products, services, or business processes introduced each year.

What is meant by strong management support?

There are a number of factors. First, there needs to be agreement among different divisions or departments that ideas will be given a fair chance. Once one member of senior management selects an idea that he or she is looking to support, other senior managers need to do what they can to support her. Senior managers need to provide people and technical and financial resources to help nurture an idea.

What often happens in today's lean work environments is that new ideas are assigned such low priority that the limited amount of people and resources just don't get around to supporting the new idea. In an organization with a strong culture of innovation, new ideas are nurtured at the same priority as ongoing business.

Business Case

In order for senior management to decide on the best idea to move forward with, one of the members of senior management should narrow the list down to three to five of the best ideas. How the best are chosen may be a result of the filtering scores, as outlined in Section 4.3, or it may be a result of personal preference. For example, if the senior manager doing the selection is familiar with certain features or services, he or she might gravitate toward those areas.

When the best three to five ideas are chosen, a business case should be written for each. In most organizations, there is a standard template for a business case document. If there is a template within your organization, follow it. If not, the business case should address the following areas: strategic context, business need, options, costs, benefits, and recommendations. The table of contents should resemble the following:

1. Executive Summary
2. Strategic Context and Business Need
3. Options Under Consideration
4. Costs
5. Benefits
6. Recommendations

Executive Summary

The executive summary is a few paragraphs explaining briefly what the rest of the document contains. The recommendation is needed at the end of the summary and should be boldfaced for maximum impact.

Strategic Context

The strategic context should outline the current situation in the organization and the strategy of the organization moving forward. This section should then outline how the new product, service, or process will enhance the current strategy.

Business Need

The business need will outline how the proposed idea will address some aspect of the business. For example, will costs be reduced by a new business process? Or will new revenue streams be added to address shareholder concerns? Or are new services being added to increase shareholder value? Perhaps it's a combination of many needs. This is often an area where the senior manager can be of most help, since he or she is often in discussions with other senior managers about business strategy and business need.

Options

When innovation ideas are submitted by employees, they may have a lot of information or just a little. The less information in the idea, the more open to interpretation it becomes. When a business case is written about the idea, there are usually several options to move forward with the idea, and each option will have its strengths and weaknesses. The top two or three options should be explored in the business case to give more meat to the idea and to allow the selection committee different options for moving forward with an idea. The options could be split by product features or marketing campaigns or anything else relevant to the idea being considered.

In terms of options split by product features, consider, as an example, the suggestion that your organization should develop a home environment control product like Amazon's Alexa or Google Home. Option one could be a similar product that offers much of the same features as are currently available. Option two could be a superior product that has improved features, such as better audio recognition and a faster response time. Option three could be a breakthrough product that offered features currently not available on either of the competitors.

Similarly, the options could be broken down by market segments. Option one could be developing a similar product aimed specifically at families with young children. Option two could be the development of a product aimed at seniors living in their own homes, while option three might be the development of a product aimed at home-office workers. In these cases, the product could be tailored to the specific market segment.

Regardless of how the options are selected, each option at this point would have to include many details in the business case at this stage of the innovation process.

Technology Push versus Market Pull

Having consulted for many technology companies and for many technology departments in nontechnology-driven companies, I have seen firsthand and several times over the difference between technology push and market pull.

With technology evolving at a rapid pace, there are many creative individuals that have thought about a new and exciting way to use the technology. Often, they get so excited about the technology, they start believing everyone will want to buy their idea because the technology is so cool. They develop new products and services, and try to push them onto the market just by virtue of how cool the technology is, or how ingenious the solution is. This is what is often referred to as "Technology Push." That is, the inventor/vendor of the product is pushing the technology on the market without the market asking for it.

Usually when technology push is involved, the end game is to find a market for the technology. The inventor/vendor tries different strategies and tactics until there is traction in one or more market segments.

Market pull, on the other hand, is trying to create products and services that meet market demand. A market need is identified, and then technology is used to try to create a product that meets the need.

There are many instances of both technology push and market pull succeeding. Some of the greatest innovations have arisen from creating a technology the market didn't know it needed. A telephone was not demanded by the public, but Alexander Graham Bell's technology created market need for real-time communication over great distances.

In terms of market pull succeeding, there are several examples where technology exists, but people want a better solution. Google's search engine was not the first search engine, but it came at a time when people were getting used to the Internet and were looking for a better way to find what they were looking for. There was a market pull for a better search engine, and Google provided a great response.

When considering options in your business case, it is imperative to have a firm hold on both the technical requirements and the market need. If the ideas being considered have arisen from a hackathon or similar prototyping exercise, then the technology may be easier to document since a prototype already exists.

On the other hand, there are business types that have a great understanding of market need but are unaware of what technology exists to address it. Getting business experts and technology experts together will allow the optimal success of a business case for organic innovation. The tricky part is getting them to speak the same language.

Each option in the business case should have its technology and business requirements well explained. This will aid in the costing of each option, as well as helping to monetize the benefits. Senior management loves nothing better than a great Return on Investment (ROI), and to get that requires monetary values of both costs and benefits.

Costs

The costs in the business case should be as complete as possible for each option. They should include:

- Product development costs
  - Human resources needed
    - Business analysts
    - Hardware engineers
    - Software engineers
    - Project managers
    - Finance, general, and administrative staff
    - Test personnel
  - Technology resources needed
    - Software
    - Hardware
    - Materials
    - Building space
    - Equipment

- Marketing Costs
  - ○ Promotion costs
  - ○ Distribution costs
  - ○ Pricing Strategy

To determine a somewhat accurate assessment of the cost, estimates should be collected from various departments, depending on the innovation under consideration. The items listed above—people, technology, and marketing—should all be considered. The people are needed in various capacities. They may be needed to design the new product, or test the new product, or manufacture the new product. Similarly, there will be people to manage the projects and to manage the money being spent.

There may also be a little amount of technology needed or a lot of technology needed. If the innovation being considered is far outside the current product range, then there may be a number of research items needed just to create a prototype. If the innovation is incremental, then there may be lots of materials available in the lab.

Marketing costs also have to be figured into the equation. To determine this, a marketing plan has to be thought out. What will be the pricing strategy? Where will the product be promoted? What is the typical buyer profile? How will the product be distributed? What will be the value proposition of the product?

An important footnote to costs is that the costs should be calculated for a full deployment. While making a prototype may be inexpensive, the costs of actually producing the product in a form that customers would buy needs to be factored in. Most of my clients separate the initial development costs from full-scale deployment costs. This is done because the initial development costs are usually fixed, while the full-scale deployment costs will vary over time. For instance, if an organization expects to sell 5,000 units, then the development costs will be calculated, and then the rollout costs will be based on selling 5,000 units. As more units are sold, there is an economy of scale. So the cost per unit goes down as the number of units increases. Meanwhile, the development costs have remained the same. If it is expected that the cost per unit is significantly different, then the cost per unit should be shown for various numbers of units.

Here is an example. I self-published my first book. The first 1,000 books were run for $10,000. Because the printer had the book set up, ready to copy, he offered me a second run of $5,000 for another 1,000 books, or $10,000 for another 5,000 books. This worked out to $5 per book if I ordered 1,000 books, or $2 per book if I ordered 5,000.

Benefits

- Cash flow benefits
  - Annual revenue increases for new products and services
  - Annual cost reduction for new processes
- Balance sheet benefits
  - Assets increasing
  - Liabilities decreasing
- Intangible benefits
  - Increased reputation
  - Increased ability to attract and retain top employees

Recommendations

In the recommendations section, there should be a chart outlining how the options stack up against each other. At the end, there should be a clear recommendation on which option should be chosen and why it should be chosen. This recommendation should be outlined and boldfaced in the Executive Summary section.

Team Selection

Each quarter, one member of senior management should be looking into the filtered ideas (from Chapter 4), and select a few possible ideas to escalate. The decision on which ideas to escalate may be made on area of expertise, area of interest, or the biggest bang for the buck.

The team helping the senior manager to decide which idea(s) would make it to the pilot stage may well depend on the substance of the ideas being considered. A beverage company investigating new bottle possibilities, for example, may require several experts: an expert in plastics, an expert in chemicals, and so on.

Regardless of the ideas being investigated, there always need to be at least one financial expert and one technical expert on the selection team. This insures that both technical and financial matters are given fair consideration.

Often senior managers are too far removed from the staff level to determine appropriate team members. Many organizations with a strong innovation culture have pools of people that can be selected from, with varying subject matter expertise. A selection committee may be needed to help senior managers investigate their ideas.

If the ideas for innovation are incremental, that is, an extension of current products and services, then it is much easier to select a team than if the ideas for innovation are explosive, that is, far outside current product and service lines.

At the beginning of Chapter 4, there is mention of a video on demand service that arose from an innovation brainstorming session at a company I worked at early in my career. When the service was being considered, there was no one in the company that had experience in video technology or the sale of video products. Selecting a team to investigate came down to choosing technical and financial experts with an interest in new products and the time to devote to the project. A member of the sales and marketing team was also brought in to investigate where possible product demand lay and to determine possible promotion and pricing schemes.

Not all members of the team need to devote their entire workday to the investigation of the new product, service, or innovation. Often, the organization's experts are the most in demand, and their time is the most precious.

In order to properly manage the selection of the team creating the business cases, there should be a project manager assigned to aid the team in defining and meeting milestones. This will help the team meet deadlines, and provide a single point of contact for the senior manager who has adopted the various ideas for investigation.

The end goal of the team is to create a business case for one or many ideas the senior manager has selected for investigation. Hence, the team should be comprised, at a minimum, of members that can contribute to various areas of the business case.

Early in Chapter 1, there is mention of three typical sections of any organization:

  i. Sales and Marketing
 ii. Operations
iii. Finance, General, and Administration

There should be at least one member from each of these areas. The sales and marketing team member can contribute to customer demand, pricing, distribution channels, and promotion techniques. The operations member can contribute to product/service development, manufacturing, and customer service. The finance, general, and administration member can contribute to budget, HR, and procurement issues.

Other help may be added as needed. For instance, there could be one sales member and one marketing member. Similarly, there could be a member each from product development and manufacturing.

The project manager should gather the team as necessary, once selected, to ensure a common goal is being targeted. Often, the project manager role is covered by a manager of one of the team members.

As with any other team, the success of this team will depend on the contributions of each team member. Younger team members cannot be dismissed by senior team members, and softer-talking team members cannot be ignored by powerfully speaking team members.

As a project leader early in my career, I was selected the leader of an innovation team that was investigating new processes for software development. There were four of us on the team, yet one of the members never contributed. He was given many opportunities to bring his ideas forward, but he just kept saying that he was in agreement with what the rest of us were saying. The other team members said that his lack of contribution was wasting time, and we should remove him. So, as team leader, I replaced him with a more active speaker, and the team moved forward quicker.

Sales and Marketing Considerations

Sales and marketing is an important factor in the success of any new product. In technology companies, there is a common misconception that great technology sells itself. So it is important to have strong representation from sales and marketing when evaluating new ideas.

The sales considerations include how the new product and service will benefit the client. There needs to be a sales process that will turn prospects into clients. The sales force needs to know what the marketing department has been promoting.

The marketing considerations include the traditional four Ps: price, promotion, product, and placement. How the new product or service will be priced is not always easy when the new product or service is a game-changer or explosive innovation. Finding comparable products is always possible, but it may take some time. Promotion and placement need to be considered. How the potential customers will hear about the new product and how they will receive the new product are of vital importance.

Financial Considerations

Financial components of the new products or services need to be considered. How will payment be collected? When will payments be made? Is funding available or will funds have to be borrowed?

For start-ups and scale-ups, there are more considerations for financing, since it is probably harder to come by. Financing innovation is always a risk, and it's necessary for business leaders to trade off the risk versus the reward.

In 2010, I interviewed Isadore Sharp, the founder of the Four Seasons hotel chain, for a *Fast Company* magazine blog. At the time, financing was hard to come by due to the recent collapse of the housing market. While it was hard, it was not impossible. I asked Mr. Sharp if financing of luxury hotels during that recession would be hard to come by, and he responded:

> For sure, it would be tough. Until the financial
> community gets back into a mode where it can support industry, it will
> be tough for anyone starting out. A year from today though, there will
> be a "new normal." There are always people looking to invest, and
> always people looking for new ideas. I don't think innovation will go
> away. We're currently in a hiatus.

Mr. Sharp was correct. The financing community did come back and investment in innovation has skyrocketed over the last few years.

Technical Considerations

Technical considerations include the technology being used for the product, as well as the manufacturing and operations components of the organization. How will the product be developed? How much time should be set aside for the product development life cycle? If it's a new service, how will the service be developed and delivered?

In terms of the operations component, how will manufacturing, if needed, be introduced to the organization? How will customer service be handled? How will complaints be resolved?

There are often company standards and operating procedures in place to handle new product introduction. Regardless of being present or not, these considerations need to be taken into account for each new product or service being considered.

Summary

Senior Management

- Why it's necessary to involve senior management
- Ingredients of a successful innovation campaign

Business Case

- Putting together options
- Determining costs, benefits, and ROI of each option

Team Selection

- Bringing together the right people
- Who's who in the zoo

Technical Issues

- Determining technical changes
- Preparing for challenges
- Mitigating risk

Financial Issues

- Costs of materials
- Costs of resources

CHAPTER 6

Pilots (Series of Successes)

Before any new product or service is deployed to the masses, it is prudent to do a trial run, or pilot project. This allows the organization to determine the viability of bringing the new product or service to market, while also gauging the customers' appetite for the product, before investing in a full-scale deployment.

Infectious innovation process

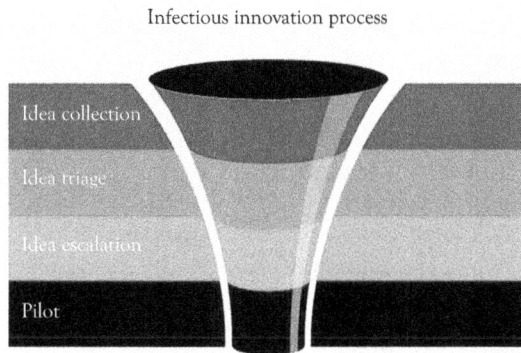

As stated in Chapter 1, some innovations are widely accepted by customers, while other innovations that are scientifically superior—for example the Dvorak keyboard—are not accepted by the market. The risk of expenditures for a full-scale deployment should be mitigated by running a pilot trial first.

An example of a pilot trial is the trial of their delivery service in Florida by McDonald's Restaurants in early 2017. *Crain's Chicago Business* reported:

> McDonald's plans to expand its relationship with Uber Technologies as it seeks to offer delivery of its food to customers in more U.S. cities.

The Oak Brook-based burger chain, which has been testing delivery through the UberEats mobile app in about 200 restaurants in Florida since December, said today it will launch delivery in several cities by the end of June.

"We're encouraged about the start we've had," CEO Steve Easterbrook said on a conference call with analysts and investors. "We are not in test mode, we are expanding."

The trial in Florida was expanded to several more cities, so it is a series of escalating pilots. They did a similar pilot in 2016 with their all-day breakfast. That pilot was so successful that it was expanded nationwide and led McDonald's to their highest stock price ever.

This chapter outlines the selection criteria, location, timing, and employee involvement in the pilot, and ends with some yardsticks to judge success.

Selection Criteria

Most, if not all, large companies have a standard set of procedures to roll out new products. The pilot phase should follow this as much as possible.

Some forethought, though, needs to go into criteria to determine where the pilot should take place, and what a successful pilot would look like. Some of the common criteria to be considered for determining where the pilot should take place are as follows:

- Which segment of the client base should be targeted
- Level of quality
- Where, if a physical location is needed, should the pilot take place
- How large of a pilot is needed to get the best confirmation
- How long the pilot should continue
- What costs are associated with the pilot
- How many internal resources will be needed to run the pilot

Client Base Segment

When choosing a pilot for a new product or service, it is important to look at which segment of your client base you wish to address. Is the new product or service aimed at a particular segment? Does the marketing team want to go across a variety of segments to determine which part of the client base is most interested in the new product or service? Does the marketing team want to try different campaigns in different markets to do a multilayer test strategy?

Different industries use wildly varying pilot strategies. Video game companies, for example, like to pilot new video games by sending out beta versions to their most avid buyers. They usually include most of the new features but not all, and usually don't charge any money. They look for feedback, and gather market intelligence before rolling out the entire product at full price. Major games, like the recently released *Tom Clancy's Ghost Recon Wildlands*, have had very successful rollouts using this strategy.

Another example of piloting to likely buyers is when McDonald's Restaurants piloted the sale of pizza in their restaurants. They chose my hometown, Ottawa, where pizza is a very popular food item. They ran the pilot for several months, but discovered that the length of time it took to cook a pizza from scratch—seven minutes—was very long for most of their clients. And many clients would change their order since their pizza would take too long. Their efforts to predict demand and reduce wait time seemed to be unsuccessful, and they ended the pilot without a major rollout to the rest of the country.

If you are going to choose just one segment of your client base to target for the pilot phase, and you are looking for the best results, target the segment that is most likely to buy the new products or services based on previous buying habits.

What Level of Quality Should Your Product Have in the Pilot Phase?

Many companies in Silicon Valley live by the motto, "Fail fast and fail often." Most companies should not adopt this motto when running a full-blown pilot. If a pilot is to predict the market's appetite for a new product or service, the best possible quality must be presented. If there is time pressure to meet deadlines while there remain issues with the product, it is best to label the pilot phase as a beta program and charge accordingly.

Today's consumers have high expectations in terms of quality of a product or service. With social media allowing most people the ability to rate and review any product or service, it's important that a new product or service is not seen as low quality. Many customers often search the Internet for feedback on new products and services, and it's imperative that the feedback is all good for new products to survive.

Physical Location

Online retailers and companies that sell exclusively to online retailers may not need to worry about where to run pilot programs as much as businesses with presence in every major U.S. market. Online retailers generally have systems set up that can ship their products anywhere in the world, so restricting their location is nearly impossible. Bricks-and-mortar companies, though, do need to consider which location is best for running a pilot program.

If there is general market acceptance in most locations, then any location could be chosen at random. The success or failure in the location chosen is likely to be the same at any other location. However, when the company's acceptance is more guaranteed in certain locations, then the area with generally the highest acceptance should be chosen. If the product succeeds here, it is not guaranteed it will succeed everywhere else; but if the product fails here, then it is likely not to work elsewhere. If a midmarket area were chosen, then the product's success or failure would not be as indicative across other segments.

Pilot Size

Generally speaking, the larger the pilot, the closer the resemblance will be between pilot results and full-deployment results. As a risk mitigation strategy, though, the pilot should be as small as possible to keep investment low until the ability of the new product or service to meet the market needs is proven.

A general rule of thumb for the pilot phase of a new product or service is to cover 10 to 20 percent of the full market. This will be a small enough investment so that total failure would not affect the bottom line, while success at this level should give enough confidence that full-scale deployment should be initiated.

Pilot Duration

The *Seinfeld* television series started with an original slate of four shows. After the first four shows, ratings were near the bottom of ratings of all television series on air at the time. It was quite conceivable that the show could have been cancelled due to its low ratings, and probably would have been cancelled if it were to start airing in today's competitive environment. However, the show continued past its initial slate and was able to continually grab more and more market share until it was number one in the market.

Hindsight is 20/20. It is easy to look back and say it was a good decision to continue longer with the innovative show to see if it could eventually garner a large market share, which it did. How long should your pilot phase be in order to determine if your new product or service will be a success or not?

There is some dependency on the product or service you are bringing to market. For example, if you were to introduce a new air-conditioning product in December in a northern climate, it will probably not catch on. Similarly, introducing a new air-conditioning product in May should not be stretched beyond any reasonable purchasing time frame.

As with location, it is best to target a time frame that will give you the greatest chance for success. Back-to-school items, for example, should be piloted in July and August when the market is looking mainly for such products.

If your new product or service has no favorable time frame, then it is necessary to select a time period that you think will represent a good sample of buyer interest. It should be long enough to help you adjust to customer feedback (like the McDonald's pizza pilot trial in Ottawa,

Canada) to see if there is a slight variance that can dramatically improve the odds of success for your new product or service.

Recommended Investment in Pilot

If the Infectious Innovation Process has been followed step by step, where ideas have been selected from a large sample and then vetted through the business case and senior management backing phases, your company should have the confidence to make a significant investment in the pilot phase of this new product or service. Most of the above criteria will have an effect on the investment needed to run the pilot, but the actual money spent needs to be monitored and focused on as well.

Investing in a pilot project needs to be significant enough to guarantee the likely outcome of the product if it were to advance to a full-scale deployment. Marketing budgets need to be scaled to meet the demand of a pilot, as well as the manufacturing costs, where applicable. The intent of the pilot is to determine if the forecast ROI will reasonably be met.

The Number of Internal Resources

The number of internal resources needed to run the pilot may influence the decision on where to run the pilot. If there is a significant number of internal resources needed to run the pilot, then it may be a good idea to select a location which is close to where a significant number of staff members work. Otherwise, the travel and accommodation costs may have an adverse effect on the return.

The seven selection criteria need to be weighed against each other. Nothing works in isolation. On the other hand, successful businesses already have many of these things figured out. They will already have a significant work force located near the biggest customers. Hence, the targeted client base segment, physical location and location of internal resources is probably straightforward if your business is sticking within your most successful product lines. If new product lines are being targeted, then it might not be such an easy choice.

Consider the selection criteria, but don't over analyze! Make your choice and move forward. There are many rewards for those who take the calculated risks.

Judging Success

When investments are made in pilots, there should be some performance criteria put in place in advance. Sales, meeting customer demand, and product returns are possible performance criteria to put in place. The number of sales measures success in promotion, pricing, and placement, as well as success in the sales process of educating the sales force and having the sales force be able to put that education to good use. The ability to meet customer demand measures success of the manufacturing and operations teams to produce the products and services in a timely manner. Product returns and customer complaints measure the lack of quality in a product. Success is typically measured by the lack of customer complaints and product returns, so there's an inverse relationship.

Expected values for sales, ability to meet customer demand, and product returns should be recorded as a baseline. As the pilot trial is run, actual values should be compared to the expected values. If the actual values are not meeting expected values, adjustments should be made. Sometimes all the adjustments in the world are not going to be able to help the organization meet its goals. In this case, there needs to be a decision to stop the pilot.

On the other hand, some pilots are wildly successful and far exceed customer expectations. A great example is the Magic Kingdom in Walt Disney World in Orlando. Disney bought 43 square miles of swampland in central Florida, and opened in 1971 with one theme park and three hotels, covering less than 10 percent of the purchased land. As the theme park became more successful, additional hotels and theme parks were added on the land. Currently, there are four theme parks, two water parks, four golf courses and twenty-eight Disney hotels on the property.

Pilot versus Rapid Prototyping

There is a lot of buzz around the term rapid prototyping. This is not the same as a pilot trial. Rapid prototyping is a set of techniques to create a model of the end product in a short period of time. When applied to software, rapid prototyping refers to creating a scale model of the software to see how it would work. This might address the technical issues, and allow senior management to see how the new product or service would look or act, but it is far from a pilot trial.

A pilot trial is much more comprehensive than rapid prototyping. A pilot trial includes sales and marketing, operations, and finance to run through the design, manufacture, sales, and distribution of new products and services. It is creating an entire ecosystem to develop, sell, and support a new product or service, but on a smaller scale than the entire market. For instance, a pilot trial of a new medical device might involve the design, development, manufacture, sales, and distribution to a large city that is representative of the expected market for the device.

Having the ability to develop and manufacture the device does not ensure the market will accept it. Having a market with a hungry appetite for the product or service you are developing does not ensure the market will rush to buy your product or service. Get real products or services developed. Put them in front of real customers, and see how it works.

With a pilot trial, adjustments can be made. Sometimes the marketing needs to be beefed up to attract the right clientele. Other times, the new product or service needs another feature or two. Pilot trials allow organizations to test on a small scale before rolling out to everyone.

Large organizations may consider a city to be a small scale, while others consider a country to be a small scale. Use discretion with the criteria listed below to determine how big your pilot should be, and how far it should stretch.

Having your organization run a pilot trial is much different from having your client ask for a pilot trial to test the product. When a client requests a pilot trial of your product, it normally indicates a lack of trust in the ability of your organization to deliver on the quantity and quality expectations.

Other times, a sales force will offer to do a free pilot trial to get the client hooked on the product. I once worked for a small start-up that was trying to acquire large financial institutions as clients. They offered to do pilot trials in an effort to show some potential clients how valuable their software was. They didn't charge the client for the software at first, while doing trials to determine what the most popular features were and how to tweak the software to best meet the client's demands. The financial institutions were happy to try the software for a limited time, but never purchased the product.

When pilot trials are discussed with respect to the Infectious Innovation Process, the intent is to run through the sales cycle as it is intended to be.

Alternatives

In modern times, there are many alternatives to pilot trials. Rather than roll out a full deployment to a test market, organizations are using different methods to determine if the features of a product are technically robust, while also determining if market demand is being met.

Focus Groups

Television shows have long used focus groups. They will show an episode or two to a focus group to gain their feedback on how popular the show may be. This is more important today than ever before. The number of scripted television series has exploded over the last few years. In 2010, there were 216 scripted television series, while the number more than doubled to 455 in 2016. This is due to many organizations taking advantage of the technological innovation of streaming video to meet an increasing market demand to binge on entertainment. With mobile devices, customers may be entertained many more hours of the day than they could have been years ago.

Focus groups can be held on a large scale. When living in Ottawa, I was invited to a focus group with 500 others to watch two different television shows. If 500 people were watching in Ottawa, there were probably thousands across North America invited to attend for their feedback.

This doesn't mean focus groups are always right. In early 2017, Pepsi produced a commercial that showed Kendall Jenner leaving a modeling gig and walking into the middle of a standoff between protesters and police. She offers one of the police officers a Pepsi, and the protesters and police all celebrate. Focus groups liked the ad, and gave feedback that the majority of the viewers were more likely to buy Pepsi after seeing the ad. When the ad was shown on television, there was tremendous backlash against the portrayal of protesters and the interaction they were having with the police. Pepsi pulled the ad the first day it aired.

Beta Testing

Beta is the second letter in the Greek alphabet and follows the letter alpha. Alpha testing is usually internal testing to test the technical and business aspects of the product, while beta testing is external testing to test the technical aspects on a larger scale and to gauge market demand for the business aspects.

Many software companies, including those in the video game industry, will ask a number of their loyal customers to beta test their software when the software is essentially complete. This allows the software company to test on a larger scale and ensure that the technical glitches are fixed before mass commercial production. It also allows the software company to determine if the features in the product are complete and meet customer demand.

Free Versions

Many developers of software applications for cell phones and tablets sell their product by giving away free versions. The free version will have limited functionality or be funded by advertising. The paid version will have all the functionality or no advertising. Market interest can be gauged by the number of users of the free version who choose to upgrade to the paid version.

Pilot Trials of New Processes

Much of the above discussion has surrounded new products and new services. This involves a lot of exterior contact—contact with suppliers, contact with distributors, contact with retailers, and contact with clients. When pilot trials are run on new business processes, the majority of work is done internally within the organization.

This requires a different mindset for the pilot phase.

The size of a pilot for a new process often seems much easier to control, but is open to office politics, especially when several different departments are involved.

In order to determine the effect of the new process, there often needs to be a baseline of the current process. The AS-IS process is often mapped, and measurements of time, resources, and materials are often taken. To map these processes, there needs to be some consideration into the maturity of the process. Processes are most mature when they are well understood across the organization and different people are following the same processes. Processes are the least mature when everyone figures out for themselves how to get things done.

If the process is deemed to be mature, then a business process engineer only needs to speak with one or two people to map out the AS-IS process. Measurements may be taken in one location and extrapolated to the rest of the organization.

However, when the processes are not mature, then the business process engineer needs to speak with several people to determine how the majority of people follow the process. Measurements need to be taken in many places and averaged out over the organization.

Once the AS-IS processes are mapped and measured, the new TO-BE processes have to be mapped out. These process maps should include who is doing what, and what information is being stored at each stage.

When the AS-IS and TO-BE processes are mapped out, there is usually a gap analysis done to determine where the gaps are between what is being done now and what needs to be done to optimize the situation.

With the gap analysis in place, the business process engineer usually develops and documents an action plan to bridge the gap. This action plan will detail a number of steps to get from the AS-IS to the TO-BE. With a mature process, this is straightforward, and the pilot may be performed anywhere. With an immature process, there needs to be some consideration of where the pilot trial of the new process will take place. Will it be done where the process now takes the longest amount of time, in order to determine the best increase in value for the new process? Or will the pilot of the new process be done where the process now takes the least amount of time, in order to determine the most conservative amount of savings?

If the current process is mature, then running the pilot should go smoothly, since everyone is used to performing the process the same way. However, if the AS-IS process is not very mature, then the pilot will have to take into account the fact that there is no consistency in place. In addition to the steps needed to move to the TO-BE state, there will also need to be steps in the action plan that serve to enforce the new process, and to provide change management services to ensure the staff involved in the process are ready for it.

When the action plan for the TO-BE process is put into effect for the pilot phase of a new process, measurements need to be taken. What resources, labor, and materials are needed to run the new processes? How does the cost of the new process compare to the cost of the AS-IS process? Often, the process will need to be performed several times to get to a steady state. The measurements should not be taken until the process is in a steady-state phase, since initial measurements will not accurately reflect the costs of the TO-BE process as there is always a learning curve to get to the new process.

The success of the pilot phase of the new process can be measured by comparing the costs of the new process once it reaches steady-state mode to the costs of the AS-IS process (which is normally already in its steady-state mode).

Summary

Selection Criteria

- Decide on Location, Timing, Expenses
- Put pilot in action

Location

- Prepare the location for the pilot
- Get teams together

Timing

- Put together project plan
- Schedule activities and possible scenarios

Who's Involved

- Select pilot team
- Lead them to success

Judging Success

- Compare Actual vs. Expected
- Forensic accounting

CHAPTER 7

Infectious Innovation Process (Putting it all Together)

Infectious Innovation is a method of transforming employee ideas into dramatic revenue growth. Employee ideas may be generated, collected, and filtered so that the optimum ideas are selected and turned into new products and services that have a dramatic impact on top-line revenues.

Senior management often tells the public that their people are the most important resource. To get the most out of this resource, employees should be encouraged to contribute to revenues by generating and submitting ideas to help the company innovate in the best possible way.

There are so many innovations entering the marketplace all the time that it's impossible for senior management to keep track of them all and to determine how these innovations may help their business move forward. It's important to allow as many people to contribute as possible so that the organization has as many ideas as possible to choose from. This allows more contributions on how the many other new innovations may impact the organization's fortunes.

Innovations do not stay ahead of the competition for very long these days. When Amazon introduced and gained traction with the Alexa home device, Google was quick to come out with its own version, named Google Home. When AMC came out with a successful show on zombies, named *The Walking Dead*, other cable channels and streaming services looked at how they could entertain clients with postapocalyptic series.

Each organization is different, despite the seeming convergence in the marketplace. They all have different strategies, but all successful organizations have the same strategy in common: growth. The best way to do this is innovation, and the best way to innovate is by incorporating the Infectious Innovation Process.

The previous chapters in this book have served to explain the various stages of the Infectious Innovation Process. This chapter details the tools and techniques that can be used to monitor and improve the success rate of Infectious Innovation.

Process Visual

Through the previous five chapters, the reader has been taken through the five stages of the Infectious Innovation Process: idea generation, idea collection, idea filtering, idea escalation, and pilots. A visual form of the process has been shown in each chapter, and it is now complete as follows:

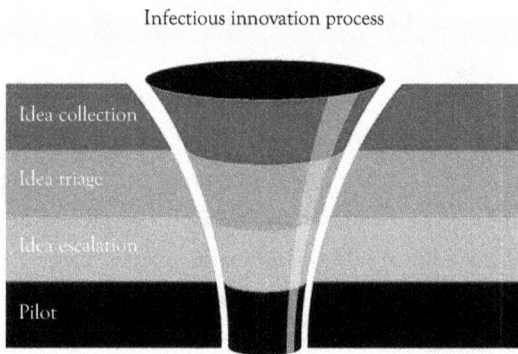

Infectious innovation process

Chapter 2, "Idea Generation," provides several techniques to indicate how individuals can use their creativity to come up with innovative ideas to help their organization move forward. The chapter ends with how individuals can expand their ideas by connecting with others in the organization.

Chapter 3, "Idea Collection," describes how organizations today are collecting ideas on innovation from their employees, be it through suggestion boxes, brainstorming sessions, innovation contests, or hackathons.

The third phase of the Infectious Innovation Process is the idea triage stage. This is described in detail in Chapter 4, "Filtering Ideas," where several methods are discussed on how senior management or the innovation committee can go through a number of submissions and decide which ones are most worth pursuing. The chapter then outlines some rating scales that an organization may use to speed up the process, while measuring against the criteria they deem important. The chapter concludes with a discussion of business strategy and how it can be used to properly triage the ideas as necessary.

The fourth phase of the process, idea escalation, is discussed in Chapter 5, "Escalating Ideas." There are many reasons given why it's imperative that someone in senior management be involved, particularly if it's a large project that will involve many departments in the organization. The components of a business case are then discussed to show how the various options may be detailed and then considered when moving forward. The chapter continues with the important aspects of selecting a team to diagnose and evaluate the various options and concludes with various financial and technical issues that need to be considered.

The fifth and final phase of the Infectious Innovation Process is the pilot stage, discussed in Chapter 6, "Pilots." The chapter specifies several criteria to take into account when a pilot is being considered. These include the client base segment, physical location, size of the pilot, length of time to run the pilot, and investment in the pilot. The chapter then outlines the timing of the pilot, who's involved in the pilot, and how to judge the success of the pilot.

That, in a nutshell, is the Infectious Innovation Process. It can be used to create new products and/or new services to help revenues grow. It can be used to create new business processes to help costs decrease. It is a systematic approach to help organizations make innovation more predictable, while optimizing the success of new ideas.

One of the most common questions is how long this process takes. There are many factors that could affect the length of time it takes. When clients are running innovation contests, there is usually a month-long intake process to allow for the submission of ideas. As organizations get more experience going through the various levels of the process, they get more adept, and the time frame decreases for the idea triage, escalation, and pilot phases.

To teach organizations how to run the process, one-day and five-day workshops are available. The five-day workshop is the preferred choice, as several hours are spent on each phase of the Infectious Innovation

Process. Participants generate ideas through a brainstorming session, filter ideas, escalate to senior management, and then decide on details of the pilot. The one-day workshop is an accelerated version where each phase is practiced through the course of a day.

Benefits

As stated in the opening chapter of this book, there is an ever-growing desire for businesses to grow. Investors are looking for organizations that are growing. Employees are looking for growing organizations. Shareholders are looking for the organizations they currently invest in to continue to grow. Many large businesses have already become global and exhausted all the possible markets and sales channels. So the best way to grow is to innovate!

The best way to innovate is to have as many ideas as possible entering a process where the ideas can be quickly filtered, escalated, and turned into pilots.

In addition to being a process that gives an organization many ideas on how to create new products and services, the Infectious Innovation Process can also help organizations to create new business processes to make the organization more cost effective. Workflows can be sped up, while resource needs may be optimized.

There are both tangible and intangible benefits of implementing the Infectious Innovation Process. A key tangible benefit is increased revenues from innovative new products, new services, or new customer relationships. Another tangible benefit may be reduced costs as new processes are introduced. In either case, there is an increased profit for the organization.

Intangible benefits include employee engagement with the growth of the company. As employees see ideas turn into new products, new services, and new processes, they grow more accepting of the process and more trusting of its ability to deliver.

Infectious Innovation Index

Every company claims to be innovative, especially to shareholders. But how innovative is a company? After working with dozens of organizations in multiple industries over the years, I have created a tool to determine how innovative a company is. It will allow a company to gauge its current level, as well as provide a yardstick for future growth on the innovation scale.

This tool is labeled the Infectious Innovation Index. It includes several indicators that show how innovative a company really is. Take the following test, and see how your company rates. As you go through the process, check after every iteration of the process to see how your score is increasing.

The Infectious Innovation Index: Perfect Score is 100

1. How many new products and/or services has your company introduced in the last year (as a percentage of total products)?
   a. 20 percent+: Score 10
   b. 10 to 19 percent: Score 6
   c. 1 to 9 percent: Score 3
   d. 0 percent: Score 0

2. What percentage of total revenues in your last fiscal year may be attributed to new products the company has introduced in the last three years?
   a. 50 percent+: Score 10
   b. 25 to 49 percent: Score 7
   c. 10 to 24 percent: Score 4
   d. 1 to 9 percent: Score 2
   e. 0 percent: Score 0

3. What percentage of expenses have been reduced by new business processes the company has introduced in the last three years?
   a. 25 percent+: Score 10
   b. 10 to 24 percent: Score 6
   c. 1 to 9 percent: Score 3
   d. 0 percent: Score 0

4. Does your company have a process to turn employee ideas into revenue-generating streams and/or expense-reduction measures?
   a. Yes: Score 10
   b. No: Score 0

5. How often does your company look to its employees for new ideas for innovative products, services, customer relationships, business processes?
   a. Continually: Score 10
   b. Once a quarter: Score 6
   c. Once a year: Score 3
   d. On random occasions: Score 1
   e. Never: Score 0

6. How straightforward is the idea collection mechanism?
   a. Simple—easy to find and easy to contribute: Score 10
   b. Fairly straightforward—contest to collect ideas: Score 6
   c. Can be tricky—everyone contributes at brainstorming session: Score 3
   d. Impossible: Score 0

7. How would you describe your company's current product line with respect to competitors?
   a. Breakthrough products/services in our industry: Score 10
   b. Superior products/services in our industry: Score 6
   c. Competitive products/services in our industry: Score 3
   d. Lags competition: Score -5

8. How would you rate the interdepartmental communication at your company?
   a. No silos—everyone is open to working with other departments: Score 10
   b. Pretty good—we all work together to solve problems: Score 6
   c. Not bad—multifunctional teams are spread throughout: Score 3
   d. What communication? Silos everywhere: Score 0

9. How many employees contribute to ideas for new products/services?
   a. 25 percent: + Score 10
   b. 10 to 24 percent: Score 6
   c. 1 to 9 percent: Score 3
   d. 0 percent: Score 0

10. How open is senior management to new ideas?
    a. Encourages new ideas constantly: Score 10
    b. Open if they see potential: Score 6
    c. Supportive if there is a clear business case with significant ROI: Score 3
    d. Unsupportive: Score 0

Answer each question, and then add up the scores of all ten questions. This sum is the value of the Infectious Innovation Index for your organization. The perfect score is 100.

A range of scores is as follows:

Over 80 points: Ideal Range. Your organization is in good shape to transform employee ideas into revenue-generating streams.

61 to 80 points: Almost there. Select one of your lower scores in the ten categories, and work on improving that.

31 to 60 points: Room to grow. Your organization has several areas to improve upon. Select two categories, and work on improving them.

30 or less points: Not very innovative. There needs to be wide-scale change to help your organization be able to transform employee ideas into revenue-generating streams.

Feedback Mechanism

An index can help you gauge how the organization is doing at a specific time. A check of how your organization is doing on the index is important to do on an annual basis to ensure that you are adhering to your own high standards.

Innovation Dashboard

There is also a need to have a dashboard to provide more frequent feedback.

The Infectious Innovation Dashboard will give an organization a real-time or near real-time indication how innovation is progressing in the organization. (Several of my clients deem reporting mechanisms that report up to the previous day as real time. Freezing results at midnight gives more comparable results over time, since the variations that occur through the day are ignored.)

The dashboard needs to capture the success of each stage of the process. It measures the success by having a few targets for each stage. Specifically, each stage needs to have an optimum target, and a minimum target. For example, the idea generation stage may have a minimum monthly goal of 500 ideas, while its optimum monthly goal may be 1,500 ideas. In this case, there would be a gauge on the dashboard for ideas generated. If the number of ideas generated in the previous month is less than the minimum, the gauge would be red. If the number of ideas generated in the previous month is greater than the minimum target, but less than the optimum target, the gauge would be yellow. If the number of ideas generated in the previous month is greater than or equal to the optimum target, the gauge would be green.

The goal for all the gauges is always the green area, or the optimum range. The red area is to be avoided, while the yellow area shows room for improvement.

The dashboard should have five gauges, one for each stage of the process: Idea Generation, Idea Collection, Idea Triage, Idea Escalation, Pilot. There is typically a sliding scale for the number of ideas as the stages progress. That is, the minimum and optimum numbers for the idea generation stage should be higher than the minimum and optimum numbers for the idea collection stage.

The entry and exit levels need to be monitored, in order to ensure maximum impact of the Infectious Innovation Process. How many generated ideas are being collected? How many collected ideas make it past the triage stage? How many triaged ideas are escalated? How many escalated ideas make it to pilot? What is the success rate of the pilot trials?

The frequency of measurement would depend on a number of variables. If an organization is running an annual innovation contest, then they would need less frequent measurement of ideas being generated than an organization that is continually looking for new employee ideas. Similarly, if an organization is triaging ideas once a quarter, then a weekly check of how many ideas are being generated would be overkill. The frequency of measurement would also depend on the frequency of meetings to discuss the innovation process.

The frequency of measurement may also depend on previous success rates of the Infectious Innovation Process within the organization. If there have been issues, and efforts have been made to improve the success of the process, then more frequent measurements may be in order.

Early in my career, I worked with a firm that manufactured telecommunication equipment. We had a responsibility to determine if incoming parts met our quality standards. A military sampling method was used. If there were no known issues with the product, then 5 percent of the components would be tested against quality standards. If any components failed the quality standards, then the number of components to be tested would be increased to 10 percent. If components continued to fail, the testing rate would increase to 20 percent, and so on. If the 20-percent mark was yielding no failures, then the testing rate would be decreased to 10 percent.

A similar system should be used with the Infectious Innovation Process. Less frequent monitoring is needed when the process is yielding results that meet or exceed expectations, while more frequent monitoring is needed when the process is yielding less than expected results.

The dashboard can be visual, by showing gauges that indicate if the output of each stage is above the optimum level, between the optimum and minimum level, or below the minimum level. Or the dashboard can be textual and merely show numbers. Most of my clients have used dashboards that combine visual and textual information to accommodate the

Infectious innovation process Q1
Collected	Triaged	Escalated	Pilot
625	398	12	2

Q1 Ideas

Collected	625
Triaged	398
Escalated	
Pilot	

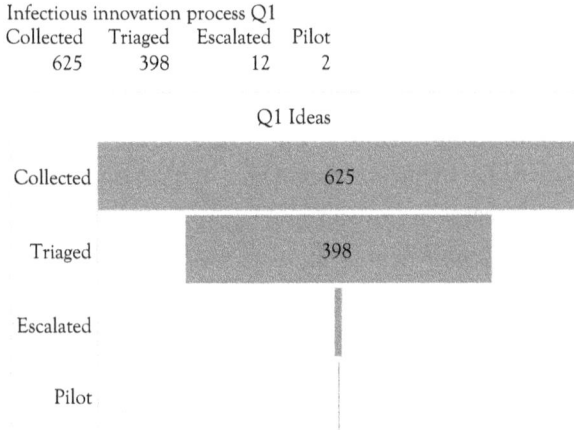

Figure 7.1 Sample funnel dashboard

varying needs of senior managers. The important aspect of the dashboard is that it allows senior management the ability to determine if the Infectious Innovation Process is running smoothly. When issues arise, the feedback can be delivered to the areas involved.

Figure 7.1 shows a funnel-type dashboard that combines the various stages of the Infectious Innovation Process. It shows both the textual and visual components of the process to accommodate senior managers who may have a preference for one or the other.

Bar charts are more popular when monthly comparisons need to be done. See Figure 7.2 below for an example. Reporting software has become so advanced that there are a multitude of possibilities.

For organizations that are committed to having a culture of innovation, these measurements can be rolled up into one measurement that can be relayed to the C-suite for consideration in their dashboard.

Length of Process

The Infectious Innovation Process is different in every organization. With the various collection mechanisms, rating schemes in the triage phase, business case templates in the escalation phase, and pilot sizes, no two implementations of the process are the same.

Infectious innovation process

	Collected	Triaged	Escalated	Pilot
Mar	315	215	12	2
Apr	283	204	5	0
May	301	189	7	1

Process Results Q1

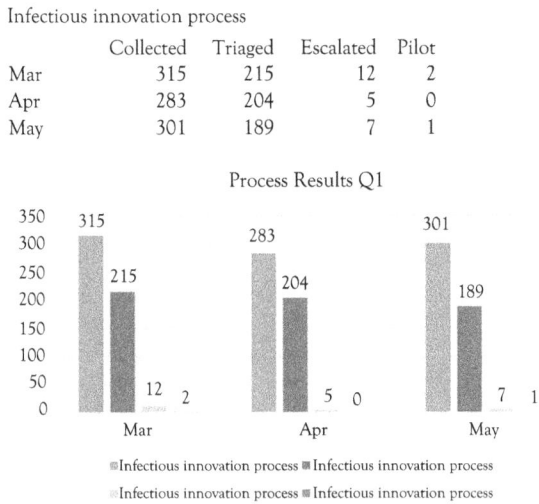

Figure 7.2 Sample bar chart dashboard

It is possible to go through the whole process in one day. Our company offers a one-day workshop, which is typically used as a trial run for the organization, but may meet all the demands if the idea generation has been done ahead of time.

A one-day workshop may also be used to address a specific problem. For example, if a client organization wants to come up with a new product to enter a certain market segment, then a one-day workshop can be held to address new products or services for that specific segment. To achieve maximum success, it is important to have a number of key personnel from sales and marketing, operations, and finance to ensure that all angles can be covered in the shortest amount of time.

A one-week workshop is more common for organizations that want to run through the process in a short period of time. This allows a day for each stage of the process, while allowing the mind to relax between each stage. As with the one-day workshop, representation from across the organization is ideal to ensure maximum success.

For organizations that want to adopt this process as part of their normal workload, the recommended time frame is three months, or one fiscal quarter. This allows for the ideas to be generated and then collected over the first four weeks of the quarter. The ideas can then be triaged over the next three weeks. The escalation phase will last for three weeks. This leaves two weeks to prepare for the pilot. The pilot then may take any amount of time, while the process starts again at the beginning of the next quarter.

Organizations that hold innovation contests or innovation brainstorming sessions typically run the contests or sessions on an annual basis. In this case, the triage and escalation phases will normally take six weeks to complete after the session or contest ends. The pilot phase will then take some time to prepare and execute.

Hackathons tend to be run on an ad hoc basis, but I have spoken with some organizations that are more proactive and schedule one per quarter. The length of time for the process to run under these conditions would depend on the frequency of the hackathons, and the outcome of the hackathon.

Getting Started

Start today! In this day and age, there is no reason to wait to grow. Investors, employees, and shareholders are looking for growth, so give it to them.

The question is never when to start, but usually how or where to start. Should your organization set up a suggestion box? Or is an innovation contest or hackathon better?

Some people are eager to be the first to try things, while others want to wait to see if the initiative has legs or is just a passing phase in the organization.

One of my clients was a telecommunications giant, and the manufacturing team was moving from Florida to Mexico. The product I was working with for the client was set to be the first one on the new manufacturing line in Mexico. The management team was not happy that their product was the first to be manufactured in the new plant in Mexico. There were unknowns in the new site, and kinks to be worked out. But one product had to be first!

The Infectious Innovation Process has the potential to dramatically improve an organization's revenues by selecting the best employee ideas and turning them into new products and services. The question I'm often asked is how to get started. The steps to follow are outlined below.

1. Determine business goals of organization
2. Determine basics of process setup: how many people will be involved at each of the latter stages, who will be involved, measurements of success for the Infectious Innovation Process
3. Set up collection mechanisms
4. Advise employees on how to contribute ideas
5. Determine grouping systems for the collection and triage stages
6. Determine rating systems for triage stage
7. Set up dashboards to provide feedback

Getting started is sometimes the hardest part. In my *Fast Company* interview with Isadore Sharp, I asked Mr. Sharp what advice he had for today's entrepreneurs, and he had the following to say:

> We all really do know what our skills are, and what
> we are gifted at. You've got to follow your passion of the moment
> (passions change over time). Let the passions be your guide, and let
> your skills direct what you want to do. Don't try to become someone
> who you are not. There always comes a time when you're at a point
> where you have to make a major life decision. Look at your passion
> of the moment.
> Don't try to plan your life, rather take opportunities as they arise. We
> all have capacity to do more. Look for the opportunities that allow
> you to do that.
> People in poor countries like India are born into abject poverty and
> can't get out because they don't get the opportunity. We are
> fortunate to live in North America where opportunity is plentiful.

I wish all the readers the best of luck as they explore the many opportunities that are out there, as they adopt Infectious Innovation in their organization!

Visit my website www.infectiousinnovation.com to get updates, and send me your success stories at james@shmconsulting.net.

Summary

Infectious Innovation Process

- Idea Generation
- Idea Collection
- Idea Triage
- Idea Escalation
- Pilots

Benefits

- Tangible: Increased Revenues, Decreased Costs, Increased Profits
- Intangible: Feeling of Contribution, Feeling Part of the Organization

Getting Started

- Start Today
- Plan the work, and then work the plan

Infectious Innovation Index

- Score the organization against the criteria
- Aim to improve

Feedback Mechanism

- Innovation Dashboard
- Improve Dramatically

Index

OTHER TITLES IN THE HUMAN RESOURCE MANAGEMENT AND ORGANIZATIONAL BEHAVIOR COLLECTION

- *Life of a Lifetime: Inspiration for Creating Your Extraordinary Life* by Christoph Spiessens
- *The Facilitative Leader: Managing Performance Without Controlling People* by Steve Reilly
- *Human Resources As Business Partner: How to Maximize The Value and Financial Contribution of HR* by Tony Miller
- *The DNA of Leadership: Creating Healthy Leaders and Vibrant Organizations* by Myron Beard and Alan Weiss
- *How to Manager Your Career: The Power of Mindset in Fostering Success* by Kelly Swingler
- *Deconstructing Management Maxims, Volume I: A Critical Examination of Conventional Business Wisdom* by Kevin Wayne
- *Deconstructing Management Maxims, Volume II: A Critical Examination of Conventional Business Wisdom* by Kevin Wayne
- *The Real Me: Find and Express Your Authentic Self* by Mark Eyre
- *Across the Spectrum: What Color Are You?* by Stephen Elkins-Jarrett
- *The Human Resource Professional's Guide to Change Management: Practical Tools and Techniques to Enact Meaningful and Lasting Organizational Change* by Melanie J. Peacock
- *Tough Calls: How to Move Beyond Indecision and Good Intentions* by Linda D. Henman

Announcing the Business Expert Press Digital Library

Concise e-books business students need for classroom and research

This book can also be purchased in an e-book collection by your library as

- a one-time purchase,
- that is owned forever,
- allows for simultaneous readers,
- has no restrictions on printing, and
- can be downloaded as PDFs from within the library community.

Our digital library collections are a great solution to beat the rising cost of textbooks. E-books can be loaded into their course management systems or onto students' e-book readers. The **Business Expert Press** digital libraries are very affordable, with no obligation to buy in future years. For more information, please visit **www.businessexpertpress.com/librarians**. To set up a trial in the United States, please email **sales@businessexpertpress.com**.